Serial Killers *of* Russia

Case Files from the World's Deadliest Nation

Wensley Clarkson

WELBECK

Published by Welbeck
An imprint of Welbeck Non-Fiction Limited,
part of Welbeck Publishing Group.
20 Mortimer Street,
London W1T 3JW

First published by Welbeck in 2021

A CIP catalogue record for this book is available from the British Library

ISBN
Paperback – 9781787396029
eBook – 9781787396104

Typeset by seagulls.net
Printed and bound in the UK

10 9 8 7 6 5 4 3 2 1

www.welbeckpublishing.com

CONTENTS

There are no serial killers here. Serial killers are an American inven-
tion, a Western decadence that could never exist in our motherland.

Politburo member just before the fall
of the Soviet Union in 1988

"Remember this, every son, know this, any child, any son will
grow into a pig if he starts out as a piglet."

The boy went away happy and Munchkin decided: "I will do
good, and not bad!"

Vladimir Mayakovsky, Soviet poet, 1893–1930

THE AUTHOR

Wensley Clarkson has investigated and written about many crimes – including serial killings – across the world for the past 40 years. His research has included prison visits, surveillance operations, police raids and post-mortems. Clarkson's books – published in dozens of countries – have sold more than two million copies. He has also made television documentaries in the UK, US, Australia and Spain and written TV and movie screenplays. Clarkson's recent book *Sexy Beasts* – about the Hatton Garden raid – was nominated for a Crime Writers' Association Dagger award.

www.wensleyclarkson.com

DEDICATION

Many of the scenes in this book are extremely graphic because it is essential not to sanitize the violence in order to convey the brutal reality of being a serial killer's victim. We should never forget or ignore what these innocent people went through during the last awful moments of their lives.

For that reason, I dedicate this book to *all* the victims of the serial killers of Russia, a nation whose beauty has been scarred by so many decades of violence.

You are not forgotten.

AUTHOR'S NOTE

The real truth about many of these gruesome murders is exposed here for the first time in defiance of the veil of secrecy thrown over these crimes by the Soviet Union and its successor, Putin's Russia.

However, I've occasionally had to deduce certain aspects of these events in order to ensure each story flows from a dramatic perspective because my main aim is to enhance rather than detract from the impact of these horrifying murder stories. This means that, while all scenes have been inspired by real circumstances, occasionally dialogue has been expanded, and certain names and locations have been changed out of respect for the victims and their families.

I make no apologies in advance to those of you who are squeamish about such graphic scenes because there is no way to water down what these killers have done.

These stories provide a unique perspective into a deadly nation through page-turning prose intended to grip readers from the start to finish of each case. The accuracy of the murders themselves, their causes and their consequences is irrefutable.

INTRODUCTION: IN THE EYE OF THE STORM

To understand a serial killer's motivation, it's crucial to get beneath their skin and find out what makes them tick. In this book, I've reported their crimes but also unpeeled the lives of these murderers by revealing events that so clearly contributed towards turning them into psychopaths.

Over the past 30 years, I've encountered male and female serial killers in prisons across the world while researching my books and TV documentaries. Most struck me as empty, soulless characters who obviously lacked empathy and, more often than not, charisma. By the time I talked to them, they'd mostly been broken by the reality of facing a one-way trip to the execution chamber or the rest of their lives in prison. I concluded that Hollywood's enigmatic Hannibal Lecter-type version of serial killers was a long way off the personalities of the real murderers. That is, until I found myself working and living in California in 1995.

One morning, my agent called me about meeting some-one who had a "unique book project" at a small, rundown dive bar just off Hollywood Boulevard, in the centre of Los Ange-les. When I asked my agent who the subject was, he laughed and told me all would be revealed when I met him. Three hours later, I was sitting in a shabby, threadbare maroon velvet corner booth in the far end of the bar when my agent walked in alongside a man with flowing blond hair and a beard. Dressed like a fashionable lumberjack, complete with denim jacket, checked shirt and jeans, he resembled a laid-back young Cali-fornian university professor. The pair headed straight to where I was sitting. We shook hands, and he refused an offer of a drink, sat down and then introduced himself. Up until that point, no one – including myself – in the tavern that day had the vaguest notion he was the nation's most wanted man.

Glen Rogers, aged 33, was on the run and wanted in connection with at least half a dozen random killings of women. Millions of Americans were transfixed by the tele-vised nationwide hunt for him because he didn't fit the usual profile of a serial killer. He'd just been nicknamed by the media as "The Cross Country Killer" (because he was on the run heading west across America) when he plucked my literary agent's name out of the Hollywood yellow pages and phoned him. Rogers wanted someone to write his life story before he was either arrested or mowed down in a hail of police bullets.

Three elderly drunks downed bourbon shots at the main bar as a scratchy old jukebox next to us blared out "Riders in the Storm" by The Doors. Rogers then carefully placed his hands down on the table between us as if to assure me he was not armed, and then he began to speak.

"Please don't judge me," said Rogers quietly, while constantly panning his eyes around the dimly lit bar to see if anyone had recognized him. "I want folks out there to understand how I became this person. Things happen in your life – especially when you're a kid – and those events send you in one of two directions. I went down the road marked The Devil and from then on I didn't care who I hurt. People meant nothing to me. They were just objects that got in my way. I didn't consider them as flesh and bone. They were just stopping me from having what I wanted."

What followed were allegations by Rogers of a harrowing, abuse-filled childhood filled with unimaginable horrors. He talked about being sexually abused and abandoned. As he spoke, tears welled up in his eyes, and it was clear he meant every measured word that he was saying.

The reason for mentioning Rogers here is that I never forgot his words. I have no way of knowing if his specific claims were true because his book never materialized. A few days after that meeting, he was arrested following a dramatic 13-mile police car chase on the outskirts of Waco, Kentucky. But meeting Glen Rogers in person that day made me fully appreciate for the first time that what so often happens to serial killers before they cross that line is as important as the crimes they ultimately commit. And that is one of the main reasons why this book reveals so much about the backgrounds and damage that turned many of these individuals into psychopathic killers, as well as outlining their appalling crimes. The soul was starved and beaten out of many of these characters before they were old enough to read and write. As a result, they grew up unable to relate to the emotions most of us take for granted.

Many of the Soviet Union's state-appointed psychiatrists during the nation's communist rule insisted that all mass murderers had been born to kill and that there was little that could be done to prevent them from committing their heinous crimes. These experts shrugged their shoulders and gave the impression that "people hunters", as they called serial killers back then, were in their country to stay. But what is it about the nation's psyche during those often-harsh Soviet times that made these homicidal criminals believe they could get away with mass murder?

One answer may be suggested by my experiences during a visit I made to Vladimir Putin's home city of Leningrad (now St Petersburg) back in 1965. I was with my mother on a 10-day holiday. It seemed an unwelcoming, grey, lifeless sort of place back then, where few tourists ever dared to venture. As a nine-year-old English schoolboy, I was looked on as something of a novelty by hotel staff. Out on the often-deserted city streets, no one seemed prepared to look me in the eye, let alone smile. But that strange vacation has remained embedded in my memory for one much more significant reason. It cuts right to the heart of this troubled nation.

On the fifth day of that holiday in Leningrad I was trapped in a broken-down hotel elevator with six Russians for eight hours. No one said a word to try and reassure me that everything would be okay. I clearly remember that it felt as if those adults in the lift with me didn't dare shout for help or bang on the walls to get us rescued. It was as if all the spirit had been knocked out of them. Even when we were finally rescued, they simply trooped stony-faced out of the hotel as if nothing had happened. It has always stayed with me that citizens back then just kept their heads down and tried to avoid challenging authority. No wonder so many serial killers began emerging from the Soviet Union around this time.

Communism itself had been sold to the Russian people as the answer to all their problems. It was supposed to mean equality for all. A fair and even-minded society where people could go about their business and enjoy a safe, healthy life. It never turned out that way. Some of the serial killers featured here were undoubtedly victims of the failure of that political system, which had been so readily adopted by idealistic twentieth-century revolutionaries, some of whom turned into despotic, power-crazy dictators and bullies. The new Russia that emerged in the 1990s from the ashes of the old communist regime wasn't much better, either. It was riddled with corruption, and many of the attitudes that dominated the old Soviet regime still exist to this day.

Rest assured; this book is not going to come up with lame excuses for the abysmal crimes committed by these serial killers. However, my investigations into the background of some of the murderers featured in this book have exposed why so many of these killings were not properly investigated at the time they occurred.

Police in Russia refused to contemplate that some of the killers in their midst could be women. The macho, table-thumping, vodka-swilling, arm-wrestling typical Russian male back then, a type prevalent in police forces, believed that women – the supposedly weaker sex – were not capable of such heinous crimes. As a result, a number of female serial killers continued their reigns of terror for much longer than their male counterparts. This, despite the fact that they should have been easier to track down because they tended to kill people they knew, often for financial gain and because they needed to "gather" resources to provide for their offspring.

Yet when Soviet police officers and their Russian successors finally chose to acknowledge that some of these killers were female, they denigrated them by giving them cheesy nicknames like "Jolly Jane" or "Tiger Woman". The clear inference was that their gender made them more "amusing" and less harmful than their male equivalents.

PROLOGUE: WHEN THE DAMAGE WAS DONE

So what made the collective Russian psyche what it was? Many remain convinced that centuries of struggles between the forces of good and evil left this proud country in a murderous fury, angry at the suffering it had been exposed to for so long. However, there is one specific period in Russia's recent history that deadened the minds of so many and changed their mentality for ever.

At least 20 million Russians perished during the Second World War – making it many more times deadly to come from that nation than any other during the conflict. When Hitler's armies surged into Russia in 1941, its citizens found themselves trapped, hungry and under constant bombardment from the Germans. And as the days turned into weeks, months and years, and with winter temperatures often dropping to minus 40, many perished from starvation and the cold.

Hitler knew the Soviet Union would be difficult to conquer but ordered his armed forces to divert manpower and artillery to the Eastern Front on a huge scale, convinced that if he took over Russia then he would go on to conquer the world. Dozens of Wehrmacht divisions, each with more than 10,000 men plus thousands of tanks and guns, supported by packs of combat planes and bombers, pulverized the Soviet Union. They specifically targeted the nation's food supplies by blitzkreiging factories and strafing convoys of trucks trying to get food to citizens in the most isolated regions.

By the autumn of 1941, the Soviet Union was left with less than three months of food supplies. Red Army soldiers on the Eastern Front were broken and starving. Food rations throughout the rest of Russia were down to a few hundred grams per day for manual workers and even less for other civilians. Bread handed out to the population was blended with sawdust to make it seem filling. When German bombs destroyed food storage units and sugar was melted into the ground by the explosions, desperate citizens resorted to digging up the sweetened earth, then mixing it with flour and cooking it. Murders were often committed in order to steal other people's ration cards. Families took dead loved ones to ration stations and pretended they were still alive so they could claim their rations. Those in charge of dishing out those meagre rations often stole food for themselves – or exchanged it for sexual favours.

Eventually, a large number of Russia's citizens were reduced to walking skeletons. Corpses began to litter the streets of most cities. As one eyewitness, Aleksandra Liubovskaia, wrote:

"People are shrivelled up, their breasts sunken in, their stomachs enormous, and instead of arms and legs just bones poke out through wrinkles." One teenager in Leningrad admitted in a letter to his own father: "I'm becoming like an animal. There is no worse feeling than when all your thoughts are on food."

No wonder some of those who remained alive began to do the unthinkable and eat the bodies of the dead. Mothers smothered their youngest children to provide human meat for their older offspring. Some husbands killed their wives to feed their children and other relatives.

Eventually, special police units were set up in the centre of most war-ravaged cities to combat cannibalism. But they still struggled to prevent citizens from eating the dead, and sometimes killing the living, in order to survive. Tens of thousands of people were arrested for cannibalism during the first three years of the 1940s. Many continued doing it even after the Germans finally retreated in early 1943. And some of those who were arrested for eating other humans were sentenced to death. The spectre of cannibalism had been ingrained in the lives of so many Soviet citizens by the time the war ended that they believed it was the only way to survive.

Today, Russia has many bustling modern cities, and there are few reminders of the suffering that occurred seven decades ago. But for at least 30 years during the second half of the last century, it turned into the most damaged nation on earth. During that period, the world assumed that America was the home of serial killers. Newspaper headlines and TV news bulletins gave the clear impression that such mass murderers thrived most of all in the supposedly decadent United States.

Criminologists have since discovered that Russia and its communist predecessor the Soviet Union had become a secret breeding ground for serial killers, decades before its enemies in the West. Data recently compiled by world-renowned criminologists has uncovered an unprecedented outbreak of serial killings in Russia, which began in the late 1960s and has continued well into the twenty-first century.

Antiquated police investigative techniques, combined with an authoritarian regime hell-bent on never revealing negative aspects of their country, contrived to keep Russia's secret serial killers out of the public eye. Law enforcement in the latter days of the old Soviet Union lacked the large-scale computerized databases that would have linked so many of the multiple killings that have tainted this nation for so long. DNA fingerprints – which helped solve so many serious crimes in the Western world from the late 1980s – were considered an unreliable Western invention by the Russians until the end of the 1990s. Others, more recently, have blamed Russia's lack of CCTV cameras for having enabled many of these blood-thirsty killers to stalk their prey without ever being spotted. In the West, CCTV monitoring is far more commonplace, and criminologists believe it has been a huge deterrent for potential serial murderers in recent decades.

Russia's police have also played other disturbing roles in aiding the nation's serial killers to remain at liberty. Overt corruption and a general disdain for the lives of many supposedly "low-life" victims undoubtedly helped spread serial killing across the country. Russian law enforcement is also notorious for its obsession with making arrests, regardless of guilt or innocence. Over-zealous police officers are known to have regularly forced confessions out of innocent citizens suspected of being serial killers. Some ended up being executed before the real killers were ever brought to justice. The message is loud and clear: you don't want to be arrested by Russian police because they're capable of framing you for a crime just to keep their bosses happy.

No wonder the Russian serial murderers who were finally brought to justice said after their arrests that they knew only too well that the police were unlikely to ever catch them. The state-controlled media also played a role in this cover-up. They were often not allowed to publish or televise details of these types of mass murders. Poor lines of communication, broken social services and an inbuilt fear of upsetting the authorities helped Russia maintain its dirtiest secret of all for decades.

Today's supposedly bold new capitalist Russia stubbornly refuses to release the details of many serial killings committed within their borders because they continue to be embarrassed by the failings of their predecessors and the perception of Russia in the eyes of the rest of the world. "Russia overtook the United States as the world's serial killing capital long ago," one renowned criminologist recently told me. "It's only now we're gradually learning the truth about so many of these abysmal crimes."

Serial killing is like Russia's own mini-pandemic. For years, the authorities covered up many of these random murders in the mistaken belief that a lack of publicity would deter other potential serial killers emerging from the shadows because they wouldn't have the oxygen of publicity to encourage them to commit their heinous murders. This approach has actually had the opposite effect, as many Russian detectives didn't even bother to mount proper investigations to bring these killers to justice because there was so little pressure from the public to catch them.

Not much happens in today's Russia without President-for-life Vladimir Putin's approval. Inside the Kremlin, it's been said that in recent years he personally encouraged the nation's police chiefs to continue ignoring most serial killings because revealing them in public would give his beloved country a bad name. There have been allegations that a number of Russia's most prolific serial killers have been tracked down by Putin's secret agents and offered freedom in exchange for carrying out executions on behalf of the state.

And then of course there is the vast size of Russia, which helped turn it into the ultimate playground for so many serial killers. The deserted landscape and huge distances between cities provided many of these killers with a perfect escape route, as well as the ability to confuse inter-regional police forces who struggled to co-operate with each other and who tend to reject ultimate responsibility for each slaying. As one California-based FBI profiler of serial killers explained: "Russia ticks all the right boxes for serial killers. Vast open spaces. Inefficient law enforcement. An often cold, dismissive response when it comes to the death of the innocent. I'm certain the serial killings we now finally know about in Russia represent no more than 20 per cent of all such murders in recent times."

From what we do know, this book chronicles some of Russia's most gruesome, disturbing serial killings. For many years after they were committed, these killings were hidden from the world by paranoid politicians and law enforcement agents embarrassed by their inability to take these psychopaths off the streets – though if they had done so, it might well have helped save many innocent lives.

CHAPTER ONE

TWISTED

Nevinnomyssk, Soviet Union, Winter 1963

The Soviet Union had more motor vehicle accidents involving pedestrian fatalities than anywhere else in the world. During that communist era, there was little regard for the safety of those on foot. Pavements were cracked and uneven, if they existed in the first place. Most citizens had to walk on the side of busy highways and just hope that passing vehicles would avoid them before it was too late.

So when a motorbike mounted the pavement in the industrial town of Nevinnomyssk, in the winter of 1963, and mowed down a young pedestrian, the reaction of those present was to simply shrug their shoulders and ignore the plight of the victim sprawled out on the pavement. He was hemmed in underneath the buckled front wheel of the lumbersome machine after its drunk driver fell asleep and lost control. The victim – a teenage boy dressed in the uniform of the Young

Pioneers, the Soviet version of the Boy Scouts – gasped for air and tried to cry out for help. Few glanced in his direction.

But there was one onlooker – a thin male in his early twenties with short hair and sunken bloodshot eyes – who was so transfixed by what he saw that he stopped to watch it all. A handful of other pedestrians recalled seeing that man and how he "seemed to be in a trance". One witness explained: "He was virtually frozen to the spot as he crouched and watched it all from the sidewalk. I remember him well because he seemed completely oblivious to everything else around him. Then I noticed that he was shaking. I thought it was fear and shock from what he'd just seen. Then I moved closer and realized what he was doing."

That male pedestrian was crouching under an overhanging tree fondling himself while studying the young boy in the scout uniform struggling for breath lying flat on his back underneath the bike. The same man later admitted that his sexual excitement had been heightened by the fact that so many people were ignoring the tragic accident, which enabled him to masturbate without anyone interrupting him.

The man said: "That boy looked so helpless, especially in his uniform. I couldn't stop studying his face and his eyes. It reminded me of how I felt inside myself after a childhood of pain and suffering. Each time he cried out in agony I became more excited. It was something I'd never experienced before in my life. In the end, I became virtually oblivious to everyone else, apart from that boy."

As petrol seeped from a gaping split in the bike's fuel tank, the man also began inhaling the smell of the gasoline as if it was perfume or a bunch of flowers. Then a small fire ignited next to the bike, and that sent him into an even more intense frenzy. After the man had climaxed, he simply stood up and walked off in the opposite direction as police sirens whined in the distance. Other pedestrians looked away awkwardly when they noticed the dark stain on the front of his trousers. But he didn't care.

A police car and ambulance arrived at the scene of the accident just as the drunken motorbike rider finally scrambled to his feet and began running in the opposite direction. None of the policemen bothered to give chase. They also ignored the two paramedics crouching next to the teenage boy, his body still trapped underneath the front wheel of the bike. It later emerged that the driver was known to the police officers because he was a relative of one of their colleagues and that they'd deliberately let him escape from the scene.

The young man who'd watched it all continued walking as he heard the police ordering people to stay back. When he glanced behind him to see what was happening, he noticed one cop directing traffic around the boy's body, which was still trapped under the bike. It was clear from the boy's open, staring eyes that he was dead.

The man felt another shiver of excitement go through his body but knew he could not return to the scene, as the police were close by, preventing anyone from taking a closer look at the grisly scene. So he walked another 20 or 30 yards further up the street and then stopped to watch from an empty bus stop shelter, where he sat down. He was fixated by the boy's open eyes staring into the cloudy sky and thought about the pain he must have suffered in the moments before he died.

The man later claimed that that bizarre afternoon was a sexual awakening for him. He insisted that, from that moment on, he knew he wanted to replicate those feelings over and over again. What he'd witnessed had empowered him unlike anything he'd ever experienced before in his life. The sight of a person dying, the smells, the fire, the boy in his Young Pioneers uniform, the crisp white shirt, polished shoes and slim tie.

The man would return to that shocking scene inside his head over and over again for the rest of his life as he attempted to replicate that same heightened level of sexual arousal. Many years later, he explained it all in these clinical terms: "I felt attraction to boys for the first time in my life. There was a lot of blood and gasoline on the asphalt. The smell of gasoline and fire. I suddenly felt a desire to hurt a young boy like him."

Like most things in the Soviet Union at that time, this tragic accident was something that no one wanted to take responsibility for. The nation's ongoing obsession with secrecy no doubt helped encourage this attitude. Most citizens back then simply wanted to survive, without the state trying to lock them up for defying the rules. And the way that all the other pedestrians had ignored the man as he masturbated gave him a newfound belief that he could get away with anything. Most citizens were too scared to pass comment. They just lowered their heads and continued their journeys to and from the factories where so many of them worked.

That year – 1961 – more than 40,000 pedestrians died on Soviet roads, though many believe the true figure was much higher than that because the obsessively secretive communist government deliberately under-played such statistics. They were determined not to taint their political system and provide their enemies in the West with anything negative to throw back at them.

The tragic accident and the sexual awakening of the young man became more significant than most other accidents on Russia's deadly roads because it also helped unleash a homicidal killer, a monster who believed he was in the hands of a higher power. The same young man blamed communism and corruption for causing the death of the young pedestrian more than the drunken motorcycle driver. The driver had friends and relatives in high places, so when he'd stumbled through the crowds he knew the police would help him cover up his role in the accident. "I had no doubt that he'd either bribed the police or was known to them. Maybe he was a policeman?" the young man recalled. "That's what it was like back then."

Anatoly Yemelianovich Slivko had just stumbled into his innermost sexual desires after a horrendous childhood that had left him jaded, untrusting and completely lacking empathy. His life would become a never-ending quest to relive that horrific traffic accident scene over and over again.

* * *

It's crucial to follow the pathway of a serial murderer right from the day they were born, if we are to get a full picture of the person and a proper handle on how and why they became addicted to killing. In the case of Anatoly Slivko, the journey through the early stages of his life was littered with problems ranging from starvation and war in his town to isolation and abuse at the hands of adults.

He was born on 28 December 1938 in the Soviet oil town of Izberbash in Dagestan, near the Caspian Sea. This bordered Ukraine, which was at that time still recovering from a devastating famine three years earlier. Slivko was a weak, sickly and emaciated child who didn't eat enough to gain the energy or strength required to fight off most ailments. He also grew up suffering from severe insomnia. Many parents from the region had themselves been so starved as children that they'd completely lost the ability to know how much to feed their young ones.

The young Slivko was also found to be suffering from hydrocephalus (water on the brain). This had given him several genital-urinary tract issues, which included bed-wetting and, later, as an adolescent boy, erectile dysfunction. As a result, he was deeply ashamed of himself from an early age. He rarely ventured out except to school and led an isolated, solitary life with few peers during his early years.

That loneliness manifested itself in Slivko's awkwardness in the presence of others, including his own family. At school, whenever he wet himself it caused him further humiliation, and he became even more reclusive. Classmates avoided him in the playground and at meal times. As a result, he soon evolved into the ultimate loner. He had no one to bounce his innermost thoughts off, so his own imagination often took over and he began building fantasy worlds of his own, which seemed a much safer option than the real world.

Life in Izberbash certainly didn't help. It was a virtual desert town, thanks to there being few local industries and restricted farmland to feed citizens. Many of the town's men worked in the nearby city of Makhachkala, the capital of the region, which was more than 50 kilometres south-east.

At that time, Soviet children were specifically educated in schools to believe that their own determination, stubbornness and courage would help them change the course of their own destiny and that of the entire world. But it was all a ploy to keep them "onside" when it came to communism.

While Slivko's father was away fighting the Germans on the deadly Eastern Front following the outbreak of the Second World War, his young son was being indoctrinated in the spirit of the Soviet education system. It was drummed into him from an early age that sacrifice to the motherland was more important than anything else. Under communism, children like Slivko were brought up to embrace the cult of fighting heroes. They were also warned that there were spies everywhere, which meant that all foreigners were treated with the utmost suspicion. So when the Germans marched into five-year-old Slivko's home town in 1943, it must have seemed terrifying.

He was already surrounded by death and destruction, combined with virtual starvation and his own health problems worsening. Slivko later recalled how one day he ran out of his home fearing that German bombs were about to rain down on him and his family and found himself all alone and afraid out on the deserted streets. As he ran for his life, he didn't know if he would ever see his parents again.

That day, he ended up sheltering in a cemetery already so badly damaged by days of German bombing that smashed, half-open coffins lay across much of the graveyard, some with the bones of skeletons exposed. The young boy joined up with a group of other children in the cemetery, who were sheltering under some overhanging trees. They all knelt and prayed that the Germans wouldn't bother to bomb the same site anymore. Many years later, Slivko claimed that the cemetery was actually a Jewish graveyard and that that was why the Germans targeted it in the first place.

Minutes after their prayer session in the smashed-up cemetery, dozens of bombs rained down from the darkened skies above. Slivko tried to huddle up close to a group of four young boys, but they were so repulsed by his emaciated frame that they pushed him away and he found himself completely alone, huddled by a wall next to a split-open coffin. As he crunched himself up in a ball and tried to rock himself to sleep, he noticed the remains of a dead horse strewn across the corpse of a woman in the street next to the cemetery. Slivko said that this upset him immensely, not because of the sight of dead bodies but because he'd thought only men got killed in wars. By this time, his own father hadn't been heard from in months, so his family presumed he'd died in action like so many other children's fathers.

Eventually, the bombing stopped, but the boy remained glued to where he sat, too scared to stand up. And he couldn't get that image of the dead woman and the horse out of his head. He kept wondering if his father had died under similar circumstances. Later that same day, he made his way home to find that his mother and sister had survived. He admitted that he'd been disappointed, because he'd felt happier on his own without them.

The following morning, he was woken early by the sound of jackboots clipping the cobbled street outside his home. A platoon of German soldiers was marching past. It was the first time he'd seen them up close. They didn't look as evil and nasty as he'd heard they would be. He was especially intrigued by the beautifully designed handheld movie cameras that many of the soldiers were using to film the surroundings as they swept through his neighbourhood.

The young boy was also fascinated by the way the Germans openly laughed and smiled. This was a huge revelation to him after experiencing precious little laughter during his childhood up to that point. As one Soviet historian explained: "Most people didn't dare to smile during Joseph Stalin's reign as leader of the Soviet Union between the 1930s and the 1950s. Stalin wanted to keep everyone down and repressed so they would not rise up and rebel against him. Looking happy was considered suspicious behaviour and could get you arrested if you weren't careful."

Slivko later claimed that seeing the Germans marching on the streets near his home had actually helped lift his spirits. Also, they were so well groomed and carried with them an impressive array of armoury. Most important of all, he adored the way they smiled. Not surprisingly, all of this was very confusing for the young boy, who'd been told by his family that the Germans were brutal, evil demons who planned to cull all the locals and had murdered his own father out on the killing fields of the Eastern Front.

Slivko's admiration for the Germans didn't last long, though. He had few friends and his family preferred him to stay at home where he was safer. As a result, he began showing an artistic side to his nature, by drawing pictures of the German soldiers. But his Nazis had big teeth and ugly faces and looked like cartoon characters, and were no doubt a reflection of the confused thoughts going through his young head at the time. In fact, young Slivko felt obliged to draw the Germans as monsters, although he didn't really believe they were. By this time, he had evolved into a people-pleasing character, especially when it came to his mother, whom everyone felt sorry for because of the death of her husband on the Eastern Front.

These experiences as a young child during the war were extremely confusing for Slivko. Some psychologists today believe that these types of mixed messages contributed to the boy's inability to differentiate between right and wrong. After all, who was he to believe?

Just before the Nazis were driven out of Slivko's home town, he and two other boys from his neighbourhood were forced at gunpoint by two German soldiers to go into a nearby forest, where they molested them.

Psychiatrists who eventually examined Slivko were unable to say for sure if this incident actually occurred. It may well have been Slivko's way of trying to elicit sympathy after having committed heinous crimes. On the other hand, it may hold one of the keys to understanding what he would go on to do in later life.

Back at school, the young Slivko continued living inside his own head much of the time. Teachers labelled him a daydreamer. As a result, he struggled in class and eventually failed an entrance exam to Moscow State University. He'd thought it would be his opportunity to get away from his dead-end home town. Instead, he was called up for National

Service in the Russian army. Slivko was told by his mother that it might help him become tougher and more outgoing. But the teenager found the army no different from school. Other soldiers bullied him and ridiculed him.

In the end, Slivko was allowed to leave the army early because of his own psychological state and his ongoing health problems. His senior officers concluded that he was not suited to life in the service. There were allegations that he was a bit "soft" which implied that he might be gay, which was considered an unmentionable topic back then.

After leaving the army in the early 1960s, Slivko – in his mid-twenties – found himself increasing trying to push his sexuality to the back of his mind. He even tried to fight his urges by moving to the city of Stavropol on the Rostov Oblast, in south-western Russia, more than 500 miles from his home town of Izberbash. He got himself a job as a telephone engineer.

The city of Stavropol seemed like a teeming metropolis to country boy Slivko. It was one of the largest cities in the North Caucasus and considered the industrial and cultural hub of the region. The city itself had multiple museums, which featured everything from priceless collections of fine art to military equipment. One included Second World War tanks and entire aeroplanes stored in enormous hangers where they hung from the ceilings.

There was also a botanical garden, which Slivko would wander through at weekends when many parents were out with their children. But he decided he needed somewhere quieter and more isolated to relax, so he began going to the less populated edge of the city, where thick pine forests bordered many of the suburbs. Loner Slivko spent hours on his own deep in those woodlands. He admitted many years later that he liked to lie down on his back in the grass and think about men that he would like to have sex with. He'd go inside his head and excite himself as he lay alone in those forests. But each time he did it, he felt less satisfied and more inclined to think about turning those fantasies into a reality.

Slivko was relieved when his younger sister eventually joined him in Stavropol. She knew he was lonely and felt it was her duty as a sibling to try and help her shy, awkward brother to finally come out of his "shell". She'd heard rumours since their schooldays that he might be gay, and she believed that she could help put him back on the right track in life. She decided the best thing for her brother would be if she found him a wife, so he could settle down and have a normal life, whatever that really meant.

In late 1962, Slivko's sister introduced him to a local girl she'd met at work called Lyudmila. She warned Lyudmila how shy her brother was. Lyudmila found herself immediately attracted to him because he was different from the men she usually dated. "He seemed much more gentle than other men," Lyudmila later recalled. "That made him more of a challenge. Most men just wanted sex and treated their girlfriends like pieces of meat. Here was a man with a sensitive side. He didn't boast about anything and he had an interesting mind. He was always thinking about things."

Slivko himself later confessed that his intensity and shyness was fuelled by his continual struggle with his own sexuality. At this time, it wasn't just the Soviet Union that failed to contemplate the subject of homosexuality. All around the world, many nations outlawed it. In Russia, it was rarely mentioned, as it was considered the ultimate personal insult. Slivko knew there was no question of him tackling his sexuality. Maybe his sister was right and he had to make an effort to be normal and have a grown-up relationship.

He married Lyudmila in the middle of 1963, and shortly after the wedding – attended by a couple of witnesses and his sister – the couple moved to the town of Nevinnomyssk, 60 miles south of Stavropol. Slivko later admitted that, despite ending up being married for a total of 17 years, the couple had sex together fewer than a dozen times. Yet somehow, he still managed to father two sons with her.

Nevinnomyssk had evolved into one of western Russia's most important agricultural market towns, located on the Kuban River where it met the Bolshoy Zelenchuk River. The city also had a chemical complex utilizing nearby natural gas reserves, as well as a vast fertilizer plant that employed thousands of people. All this made Nevinnomyssk a boom town in Soviet terms, and the population was surging. It had a busy railway centre, complete with freight yards and workshops. It was also located at the opening of the Nevinnomyssk Canal, which provided irrigation to the nearby farming areas, as well as useful additional transport facilities.

Nevinnomyssk's booming economy had been helped by a new generation of Soviet leaders led by Nikita Khrushchev, who'd discarded evil despot Joseph Stalin's brutal and repressive regime and encouraged new industries and cities to expand, in order to try and improve the life of most Soviet citizens.

This was all very bewildering for a young man like Anatoly Slivko, who'd been brought up in the repressive Soviet Union of Stalin's era. He'd ignored his own sexuality to marry a woman in the hope of a normal life, but he now found himself living somewhere where people actually smiled and earned enough money to enjoy their lives.

Up until this time, Slivko had expected little from life. Now he had relative freedom, and a few weeks after moving to Nevinnomyssk he witnessed the road accident that awoke such twisted sexual desires inside him. He said that watching that pedestrian die tapped into an urge to have real sexual encounters beyond the sick fantasies inside his own head.

Slivko quickly ingratiated himself into the local community by purchasing a cheap second-hand movie camera and then making some amateur documentaries about German atrocities committed during the Second World War. This soon provided him with a solid, reliable reputation, which in turn made him more trustworthy to his neighbours and associates. He never mentioned how he'd first been inspired to use that camera by the Nazis, who'd invaded his home town and molested him.

Just a few months after witnessing that road accident, Slivko opened a youth club in Nevinnomyssk for boys, called "Chergid". Most parents were happy to leave their children under the charge of this "typical Soviet man with a heart of gold", as they liked to refer to him. He insisted his intention was to help guide the young boys in his care towards the correct way to lead their lives. Many of the children who attended the club reminded Slivko of the innocent young pedestrian who'd died after being hit by the motorcyclist. He found himself attracted to what seemed like an endless supply line of young boys.

Within a few months of opening the club, the building that housed it was destroyed in a mysterious fire. Later, it was alleged to have been deliberately started by one of his young club members, who was upset about the way Slivko treated him. There were rumours of an "incident" between him and that same child, but it was never properly investigated by the boy's parents or the authorities. Most families were completely unaware of what had happened and considered Slivko to be a good and decent man. Many helped him locate new premises for his youth club following the fire. A few months after that, he re-opened it in a new building. He was surprised to have got away with what had happened with the young boy. Now it felt to him as if he had a mandate to do whatever he wanted.

Slivko quickly formed close relationships with some of the young boys in the newly opened club. At the same time, he became even more respected in his neighbourhood after winning film-making awards for the documentaries he'd made about the war years. At the club, he focused much of his attention on boys aged between 13 and 17, who were usually short for their age, which made them look even younger.

Many parents praised Slivko for sparing so much of his time to help their children, some of whom needed extra attention due to behavourial issues. He organized hiking trips for his favourite boys in the club and endeared himself to the boys by showing great interest in their lives. He soon received numerous letters of thanks, and local communist officials awarded him honorary certificates for setting up the youth club. He appeared on local radio and TV stations, as well as regularly publishing articles in local newspapers.

Slivko also enthralled pupils and parents alike with made-up adventure stories of his time in the army. He knew that as long as he was considered a solid and reliable person-ality, no one would ever question his motives and activities.

He told the boys and their parents he wanted the members to re-construct scenes from the Second World War on a stage at the club. He said this acting would include special rehears-als beforehand that included an exercise plan, which he told the boys would help turn them into "real men".

The shortest boys and their families were convinced by Slivko that re-constructed hanging scenes would help stretch their spines to make them taller and healthier. He also claimed these exercises would help improve oxygen intake in their bodies. And all they had to do was to obey his most important rule, which involved not eating for three hours before those hanging exercises were carried out. Slivko later admitted that this was because he didn't want any of his victims to vomit during unconsciousness because that would ruin his sexual excitement.

He and his young performers would rehearse scenes of partisans being executed by Nazi soldiers on a makeshift stage at the back of club, when only Slivko and his student would be present. The children were dressed up in Young Pioneers' uniforms, complete with shiny shoes and crisp white shirts, just like the boy who had died in the motorbike accident. These child "actors" were persuaded to place ropes around their own necks by Slivko before he choked them just enough so that they fell unconscious, after having promised to resuscitate them with first aid techniques. Once out cold, he would strip each child naked. Then he'd fondle them while filming it all and re-arrange the body in various suggestive positions before then masturbating. Afterwards he'd revive them.

Within a few weeks, Slivko persuaded one young boy that rehearsals should be held in the woods near to the clubhouse because then they wouldn't be disrupted by others. As the boy's unconscious body hung from a tree, Slivko masturbated and ejaculated onto the child's shoes, which he'd placed on the ground underneath the body. When the boy eventually woke up, he had no memory of what had happened to him.

Many criminologists have since speculated that Slivko's early victims most probably went into a state of self-denial, akin to self-inflicted amnesia, so they could avoid thinking about their appalling experiences, which became deeply held secrets that they were most likely too ashamed to share with anyone else.

Slivko always maintained that he only ever intended to knock the boys unconscious. But even this was a risky activity. On 2 June 1964, Slivko took 15-year-old schoolboy Nikolai Dobryshev into the woods like he'd already done with others before him. As soon as the child lost consciousness, he removed the noose from around his neck and posed the boy in a macabre position that he found sexually arousing. Then he masturbated over the child while caressing and fondling the boy at the same time. He filmed it all on a movie camera.

Nikolai Dobryshev did not wake up. Slivko has always insisted he tried to revive him. But once he realized he'd killed him, he dismembered the child's body, burned it and buried the charred bones.

"That was sheer cowardice on his part," one detective – who investigated the murders – recalled. "He couldn't face the reality of what he'd done, so he removed the evidence so it didn't remind him of what he'd done to that kid."

Despite Slivko's claims about the circumstances behind that first kill, experts later said he'd undoubtedly been driven to ensure there were no witnesses to his appalling abuse, which meant he could continue committing his crimes.

He kept Nikolai Dobryshev's shoes to remind him of what he'd done. No one knows to this day if that was out of a sense of guilt or simply as a trophy. It's likely to have been both. Slivko claimed he got rid of all the film evidence of that first molestation and murder, having been so shocked by the death of the boy. But in fact, the murder of an innocent child fed into his warped psyche. He admitted to one psychiatrist that he'd felt much more aroused by the death of Nikolai than by any of his earlier victims, whom he'd kept alive. Slivko's excitement was further fuelled by the act of dismembering his young victim's body and setting the limbs on fire after pouring gasoline on them. This reminded him of the smells that had aroused him after he watched the young traffic accident victim dying in front of his very eyes.

The parents of Nikolai Dobryshev, Slivko's first murder victim, were dismissively informed by police that their missing son must have run away. There was no question of pointing the finger of suspicion at a supposedly upstanding citizen, so the investigation quickly fizzled out.

In May 1965 – just months after that first murder – Slivko chose Aleksei Lyosha Kovalenko, from inside the children's club, to be his second murder victim. The boy suffered an almost identical fate to Nikolai Dobryshev.

The police were alerted by Aleksei's parents. Once again, they did not consider Slivko to be a suspect, after many parents insisted he was incapable of harming a child. Detectives told the victim's family the boy must have run away like the other missing boy.

Slivko knew he couldn't keep killing children from inside the club without alerting the authorities, so he went out and hunted down further victims elsewhere over the following 10 years. No one to this day knows who those victims were or how many there were of them. As one serial killer expert explained: "Killers like him don't just stop killing. As long as they can get away with it, they will continue. I have no doubts there are many other victims out there. Most will have been classified as runaways, who went missing."

Throughout much of this period of time, Slivko also continued to abuse other boys in his care at the Chergid youth club, though without actually killing them. Most of them had no idea what he had done to them, and the ones who did refused to discuss what had happened with anyone.

In May 1975, Slivko murdered 11-year-old club member Andrei Pogasyan. This time, the missing boy's mother told detectives about Slivko's play and how he took her son away for rehearsals. The police responded by searching the clubhouse for evidence of Slivko's activities. However, they found nothing and so told the parents their son must have run away.

The police's attitude told Slivko he was not under suspicion, so he continued fine-tuning his activities. His favourite ploy had been to gain each boy's complete adoration, trust and confidence through his position as leader of the club. Many boys were in awe of Slivko and seemed prepared to do virtually anything he wanted. He'd become like the leader of a small but potent cult, who was able to order his "disciples" not to mention their "games" to anyone, including their parents.

Then there was the film footage he shot of himself abusing, and in some cases murdering, these children. He had collected a number of old cameras over the previous five years. But instead of destroying the footage as he had done following his first murder, he'd built up a library of homemade snuff porn. He viewed it over and over again for additional sexual satisfaction.

Psychiatrists today believe that Slivko hoped that watching the films would give him enough sexual satisfaction to prevent himself from killing any more real victims. But was his real motive just to ration himself so he did not get caught? One psychiatrist explained: "Those films were never going to be enough to stop him killing. He wanted that footage purely as a way to have an additional outlet for masturbation. Like so many addicts of pornography, those films fed into his need for increasingly outrageous real life acts. As a result, he wanted to stretch the boundaries over and over again."

Slivko also used these macabre home films as a way to improve the efficiency of his killings, so as to never be caught.

He once admitted to a psychiatrist that he'd learned valuable lessons from those films about how to avoid leaving any clues for the police. This further encouraged Slivko to continue his killings. At one stage, he became so irritated by the police's inefficiency that he told a colleague at the youth club that the police were idiots when they came to the premises to interview those who'd last seen his latest victim. At this stage, detectives hadn't been able to locate the remains of the missing boys, whom they still insisted must have run away. Nevinnomyssk police were underpaid and over-worked, as they are to this day. No sooner had they started one missing child investigation then another child would disappear and they would be obliged to prioritize that one.

Between 1975 and the early 1980s, Slivko also targeted children who were not members of his boys' club, as he knew that was safer for him. And by this time, he was completely addicted to murder. But throughout this entire period, he found it increasingly hard to resist abusing some of the children under his care.

In the summer of 1984, Slivko choked 13-year-old Sergei Fatsiev until he fell unconscious during a rehearsal for one of his mini-dramas. Slivko then abused the schoolboy. Fatsiev never recovered consciousness, and so Slivko disposed of his remains.

When Sergei's parents informed the police that their child had gone missing, officers insisted he had run away. But his mother decided to take the law into her own hands and began interviewing other youngsters at the club. Some boys admitted to Sergei's mother that Slivko had been knocking them unconscious and performing various experiments on them to make them grow taller. They claimed they had no actual idea what he'd done to them.

Mrs Fatsiev soon became convinced that Slivko must have been responsible for her son's disappearance, despite what the police were claiming. But when she told officers, they still ignored her plea for them to re-investigate her son's disappearance. It has since been alleged that Slivko bribed detectives not to arrest him, despite growing evidence that he'd been involved in the disappearance of a number of boys. These claims have never been fully substantiated.

Slivko believed that, without bodies, the police would continue to let him off the hook. He'd long since made sure that the corpses of his murder victims had been dismembered enough not be recognizable even if they were ever found.

In the autumn of 1984, Slivko killed another boy from the club called Vyacheslav Khovistik, aged 15. Then, in the middle of the following year, he murdered a 13-year-old boy named Sergei Pavlov, who'd disappeared after telling his neighbour he was going to meet the leader of Chergid for a rehearsal of his play.

This was enough to finally persuade police and local prosecutors to target Slivko as their primary suspect. Within days of the disappearance of Sergei Pavlov, they began much more closely probing his activities. In early December 1985, they got a warrant to raid the youth club, while undercover officers watched Slivko at his family home, waiting for a call from their colleagues to arrest him.

Minutes after entering the premises, detectives discovered there was a dark room at the back of the building. They smashed down the door to it and found tools, rope, saws, axes and many of his victims' shoes. Detectives also uncovered photographs and videos of his attacks, many of which went back more than 20 years to when his reign of terror had first begun. At the time, police didn't realize he had destroyed a lot of footage, including that from his first murder, of 15-year-old Nikolai Dobryshev, which had occurred back in 1964.

Slivko had also recorded the deaths and abuse of more recent victims over the top of tapes that had featured his earlier attacks. He'd done that whenever he became bored by what he was watching. In one piece of footage, he could clearly be seen arranging a severed head in the middle of a circle surrounded by severed feet and a pair of polished boots, which symbolized the uniform of the Young Pioneers, which had been worn by that innocent road-accident victim.

The police were told by members of the boys' club that Slivko had been carrying out his experiments on boys for decades. In the end, detectives found enough evidence at the club to connect him to the murder of at least seven children, all aged between eleven and fifteen.

Outside his family home three miles away, undercover officers swooped and

Slivko was arrested after they'd surrounded the property. They convinced him to speak to them outside rather than upset his wife and children in the house.

Slivko began confessing to the killings as he was being driven to the city's police headquarters. He admitted, almost proudly, that none of the victims were above the age of 17. During his first full police interview that evening, he told detectives that his desire all along had been to relive that road traffic accident he'd witnessed. When one detective insisted that Slivko must have feared that older boys might have fought back, he denied ever having needed to be violent with them. "They were all under my complete control," he said chillingly.

Slivko eventually helped law enforcement agents locate the remains of six of the boys he had murdered. But he was unable to find the exact spot where he'd buried his first victim, 15-year-old Nikolai Dobryshev, whom he claimed to have accidentally killed back on 2 June 1964. He was charged with seven counts of murder, sexual abuse and necrophilia.

Exactly 22 years after that first gruesome kill, Slivko finally appeared in court in Nevinnomyssk. He claimed during his trial that the seven boys who died were just unlucky, after something went wrong during his experiment on them. No one believed him and he was found guilty and sentenced to death.

Detectives remain convinced to this day that he killed many more than the seven boys he admitted to murdering.

* * *

Psychologists have since tried to analyze what drove Slivko to commit so many heinous crimes. Some are convinced that he wanted to be caught right from the moment of his first murder but that, when no one came to arrest him, he believed he needed to kill more children to ensure he would be brought to justice.

"After that first child died, he must have got quite a shock and maybe for a moment, he even thought it was time to stop his sick experiments," one criminologist explained. "But the police never came after him for that killing and he must have interpreted this as meaning no one really cared about that dead boy. So he might as well continue attacking them because it gave him so much sexual satisfaction."

Another crime expert explained: "Killing those children became like work to Slivko, in a sense. He had to keep those two very diverse versions of his personality apart from each other or else one of them might have brought the other one down so to speak. Whenever he ventured too close to crossing over between the decent family man version of himself and the sick and twisted psychopath, it must have shaken him in a sense, and that was when he was at his most vulnerable."

One detective who interviewed Slivko following his arrest recalled: "The strange thing about him is that he showed a lot of cunning to avoid being arrested for many years. But once he was in custody, he seemed much happier than he had ever been in the outside world because he was now a somebody instead of being a nobody."

Once Slivko was behind bars awaiting his death sentence, a number of law enforcement officers from other regions of Russia interviewed him in the hope he might help them get inside the heads of other serial killers, who had not yet been caught. Slivko himself was extremely keen to help the detectives, but some officers suspected this was simply a ploy to avoid the death penalty. Police admitted his help was "limited" when it came to actually tracking down other serial killers. However, he did provide a fascinating insight into the mind of a serial killer, which in turn disclosed some of the motivations behind his own grotesque crimes.

One detective explained: "Slivko closely analyzed one specific killer for a murder squad detective based in Siberia. He sounded like a professor of crime rather than a vicious psychopathic monster as he spoke to the officer. We all humoured him by allowing him to talk extensively in the hope he might slip up when it came to all the unsolved murders he'd committed." And it worked. Slivko unintentionally admitted another of his killings while trying to help detectives on the investigation. It was one of the killings he'd earlier always denied.

In September 1989, Slivko was visited in his cell on death row at Novocherkassk prison by yet more detectives asking for help catching another serial killer. This time it became clear that his only priority was to keep delaying his own death sentence by pretending to help detectives. So, within days of the meeting, authorities executed Slivko with a common form of execution at the time, a single bullet through the back of his head. Many of the families of his victims had volunteered to fire that weapon.

CHAPTER TWO

RAT POISONING

**School number 16, Minsk District, Kiev,
Soviet Union, Autumn 1986**

Tamara Ivanyutina took offence easily. In fact, she looked upon any negative comment directed at her as a personal attack and it left her so mortified that what had been said festered for days on end. Ivanyutina would become overwhelmed with hatred for those people who dared to upset her insular world.

Ivanyutina's twisted and obsessional mind had a creative side when it came to weird ways to hurt other human beings. As a child, she'd been much more prone to crying than most infants, but that was for good reason. Things happened in her childhood that left her feeling desperately helpless. She would witness violence between her alcoholic parents and then find herself the target of their twisted responses to the problems of their lives. As a result, Ivanyutina often became more angry whenever others seemed in pain.

She once said that her mother never smiled at her when she was a baby and she learned not to expect a reaction from her, or anyone else for that matter. This clearly deadened her spirit from a young age. Others said this was just a convenient excuse for the bad things Ivanyutina went on to do. There's no doubt that if a child psychologist had been available to help Ivanyutina when she was young, then maybe she would have ended up leading a more normal life. She might have gone on to great things, because she certainly possessed a highly intelligent mind. Instead, Ivanyutina more often than not found herself completely alone when dealing with the many challenges in her troubled life.

As an adult, Ivanyutina started a smallholding of farm animals with the intention of eventually turning it into a proper business. She needed a constant supply of food to feed her animals and managed to buy low-cost leftovers from local school canteens by bribing school staff on the side. But that ate into her tiny profit margins, which made it harder to earn a living from those farm animals. So in 1986, Ivanyutina applied for a job as a kitchen assistant at school number 16 in the Minsk district of the Ukranian city of Kiev – then still part of the Soviet Union – where she lived at the time. It only paid a modest salary but she'd be able to get all the offcuts of old food for free to feed herself, her husband and, most important of all, the animals.

Ivanyutina shouldn't really have taken the job as assistant dinner lady at school number 16 since she loathed most children. She particularly disliked the sound of their chirpy voices, their pranks, their running around and just about everything else about them. Many pupils soon picked up on Ivanyutina's negative attitude towards them, too. They noticed her constantly glaring at them in the dining room. The school staff also kept their distance from her because she seemed so irritated most of the time.

Ivanyutina's own poverty-stricken upbringing meant she was resentful towards anyone who appeared to have a more fortunate life than her.

She also ignored advice from the other school staff and teachers not to shout back at the kids when they teased her. She was convinced they were looking down their noses at her.

Taking home those school canteen left-over scraps of food at the end of each day was her salvation. It kept her going, in a sense. But, as time moved on, she became increasingly obsessed with taking as much food with her as possible. She began not washing the school plates, so that pupils and teachers would be so disgusted that they'd leave their food untouched and she could scoop it all into a bag and take it home. On a few occasions, she "accidentally" turned off the school refrigerator for the night, so that by morning the food would be so rotten it couldn't be served to pupils and staff and she could take that home as well.

Instead of keeping a low profile while she was doing all this, Ivanyutina become ruder and nastier to the teachers and pupils at school number 16. When one member of staff questioned her about what she was doing with the rotting food, she snapped back so angrily at them that they backed down from the argument. Ivanyutina gave the clear impression that she didn't care if everyone hated her. But what no one realized was that her anger was pushing her towards a precipice.

When school nutrition nurse Ekaterina Shcherban and chemistry teacher Natalya Kukarenko informed Ivanyutina that she was no longer allowed to take left-over school food home with her, she exploded. "How dare they stop me," Tamara Ivanyutina thought to herself. "I need that food to survive. They have no right to suddenly change the rules." So she rounded on nurse Shcherban and shouted insults at her in a tirade of fury. As a result, she was ordered to stay away from the fridge and the stoves in the school kitchen and not to touch any of the old food scraps. The nurse also told her to stop harassing children into finishing their meals quickly so she could take the leftovers.

Ivanyutina completely ignored the order and continued doing exactly what she'd been doing all along. It was then that nutrition nurse Shcherban – backed up by her chemistry teacher colleague Natalya Kukarenko – reported Ivanyutina to the local communist party school representative, known as the *partorg*. This felt like the ultimate insult to Ivanyutina. She came from a family who detested the entire communist system and felt that it had caused their own poverty.

Ivanyutina was lucky in one respect, as she was allowed to keep her job. Firing lowly staff was something that rarely occurred. Local communist party officials tended to avoid reporting workplace theft to the police in case it exposed their own corrupt activities. Instead, the *partorg* hauled Ivanyutina before the local Communist Party Committee, where she was reprimanded and given a severe warning. Ivanyutina was convinced that the only reason she hadn't been fired was because no one else wanted her "shitty" job. She pretended to take the warning seriously, but the moment she left the school building following that hearing, she spat on the pavement in disgust. This was precisely the type of communist interference that her parents had taught her to hate.

It was the middle of autumn 1986 and Tamara Ivanyutina felt that the entire school was against her. She wanted to punish them for daring to force her to pay to feed her beloved animals. There were two students, a brother and a sister, who particularly infuriated Ivanyutina by often putting school meal remnants of cutlets, chicken bones and other leftovers in a bag for their dog. Ivanyutina had reprimanded them the moment she saw them doing it. They shouted back at her and ran off. Ivanyutina considered their actions to be a personal insult. She decided, using her own strange logic, that school staff had most likely put them up to it just to annoy her.

The following day, Ivanyutina slipped drops of a poisonous fluid called thallium – also known as Clerici's – into the brother and sister's food before handing them their lunch plates. Within minutes, the pair were being put into an ambulance on stretchers and rushed to hospital with what was presumed to be stomach poisoning. As it turned out, the dose of poison Ivanyutina had given them was not enough to kill them, and they survived. She later claimed she knew exactly what she was doing and had decided it was not worth killing those two pupils. "But at least they suffered," Ivanyutina recalled, with a tone of satisfaction.

After that, she had bigger fish to fry. A few days after the two pupils collapsed, Ivanyutina switched her attention to school nurse Ekaterina Shcherban and chemistry teacher Natalya Kukarenko. She was still angry that they'd reported her to the *partorg* as well as banning her from taking any leftover food home with her. She felt they'd deliberately humiliated her in front of all the students and other teachers, who laughed and sneered at her even more after word got around the school that she had been reprimanded.

A few days after the two pupils had been hospitalized, the school nurse, Ekaterina Shcherban, had to be rushed to hospital after collapsing in the school's main corridor. Within two weeks, she'd died of what doctors insisted was stomach poisoning, which was not unusual in the Soviet Union at the time.

A few weeks afterwards – in the spring of 1987 – chemistry teacher Natalya Kukarenko was also taken to hospital. She told doctors she was suffering severe stomach pain and numbness and doctors suspected heart failure. Her condition worsened, and she too died within days.

Not satisfied with just those two, Ivanyutina targeted the school's assistant principal, who'd dared to call the repairman to fix the canteen fridge, which had prevented her from taking home more leftovers. Ivanyutina hated the assistant principal more than anyone else, as, following the death of nurse Ekaterina Shcherban, he'd also ordered that a lock be put on the pantry door and insisted on carrying the only set of keys with him at all times.

Moments after the assistant principal sat down to eat the buckwheat soup that Ivanyutina had poisoned, he was called away to a meeting. Before leaving, he poured the soup back into the pan on the kitchen counter, and it ended up being consumed by a number of pupils and staff members. Ivanyutina later described the dozen children poisoned that day as collateral damage. One staff member who was present in the canteen recalled: "Tamara was standing there frozen to the spot watching them all avidly with this awful smirk on her face. It was as if she was getting pleasure from each mouthful of soup going into their mouths."

Three sixth graders and eleven school staff were hospitalized with what doctors described as a bout of lethal flu. Their symptoms included fever, nausea, bone pain and significant hair loss. This incorrect diagnosis proved tragically costly, as four of the people rushed to hospital – including two schoolchildren, a teacher and a repairman for refrigeration equipment – eventually died.

Having so far evaded detection, Ivanyutina's next target was to be a teacher who'd been rude to her in the canteen about the same food issues that had led earlier to her poisoning nurse Ekaterina Shcherban and chemistry teacher Natalya Kukarenko. This teacher's symptoms weren't exactly the same as those of most of the other victims, which meant this wasn't connected by school or medical authorities to the previous incidents. That worked very much in Ivanyutina's favour. After some time in hospital, the teacher survived, after what had been diagnosed by doctors as a heart attack.

School officials and hospital staff remained completely unaware that Ivanyutina was systematically killing pupils and staff who'd upset her. The deaths and illnesses were still mainly labelled as influenza, despite the symptoms varying enormously. A team of respected virologists and epidemiologists informed school staff and pupils that the flu was unlike any strain of the illness they'd ever seen before. The medical experts insisted there was no other possible explanation than that it was indeed this sometimes-deadly sickness.

So, on 27 March 1987 – three weeks after the release of the teacher from hospital – the school had to be shut down for what officials were calling a "state of emergency".

When one medical expert pointed out that most flu dispersed by March of each year and speculated that maybe the victims had been poisoned, he was ignored. A few days later, the same specialist was visited by members of the local communist party and warned to keep his opinions to himself because he was causing alarm in the community.

The school was eventually reopened after flu tests on all the staff and pupils proved negative. In the canteen, kitchen assistant Tamara Ivanyutina continued serving meals as if she didn't have a care in the world. Some students and staff recalled that she actually seemed a lot happier after all the "tragedies". One pupil explained: "She was like a different person. No one was breathing down her neck anymore and most pupils had long since decided to keep well away from her as she'd been so impatient with us in the past."

Outside of the school, though, the mysterious deaths of so many in one Kiev school were noted with interest in the city prosecutor's office. Their suspicions revolved around possible faulty gas pipes or legitimate food poisoning. So investigators were ordered to open an enquiry to try and get to the bottom of what had happened.

Initial checks of the school building itself included a radiation check, after fears that there might have been a leak from a nearby power plant. When those tests proved negative, detectives interviewed those who'd survived the "sickness". They discovered that many of the large cluster of victims on one particular day had been late for lunch in the canteen and that they'd all eaten soup with buckwheat and chicken liver.

The ones who'd arrived on time for the meal had not been sick afterwards. The investigators were completely thrown by this and wondered if poison used to kill rats and cockroaches might have somehow got into the food *after* most pupils and staff had already sat down and eaten their meals in the canteen.

Staff and children complained to investigators that poor quality meat was often served in the school meals, but it was clear this was not a normal case of food poisoning, given the severe reaction. One staff member suggested to investigators that perhaps a gang of troublesome teenage pupils had deliberately splashed poison all over the food in the containers on the serving counter. Or maybe they'd put it in the water supply as a prank? Investigators ordered an inspection of the school kitchen area and they interviewed all students who did not get poisoned in the hope they might find the culprits. They all denied any involvement in the poisonings, and there was no evidence of poison in the kitchen, either.

Watching all this from a safe distance was Tamara Ivanyutina. Her mood lightened more each time she heard that investigators were failing to establish what had really happened. She adored watching all the staff and children being grilled by officers, who began openly admitting it might soon be time to close down their enquiry because there was no actual evidence of foul play.

Then, in the middle of this, investigators discovered that the body of chemistry teacher Natalya Kukarenko – who'd died a few weeks earlier – had not been examined by forensic scientists as the city could not afford the cost of the autopsy. Many unexplained deaths had simply been ignored, some would say covered up, by authorities for similar reasons in the Soviet Union at this time. The nation's leaders had for decades been encouraging this practice so that they would not be connected to the numerous illicit killings carried out by the state. The communist regime had literally been getting away with murder and this had, in effect, helped many killers get away with their crimes.

Back at school number 16, Ivanyutina was feeling happier by the hour. Staff and children noticed she'd taken to singing and whistling tunes to herself as she served food to everyone in the canteen with a broad smile on her face. As one pupil explained: "Yeah, she'd once been a scary looking, grumpy old lady but that didn't make her a killer. In any case, back then we were more worried there was a epidemic going around the school. None of us realized those people had actually been murdered."

While interviews continued, chemistry teacher Natalya Kukarenko's corpse was exhumed and sent for examination at the city morgue. Within hours, traces of thallium were found in the tissue of her remains. It was only then that the Kiev coroner finally announced that some of the victims might have been poisoned and the police actually launched a proper murder investigation. The finger of suspicion, however, was not pointing anywhere near Ivanyutina.

Instead, detectives were focusing their attention on a teenage pupil renowned in the school for his almost obsessive love of chemistry. He'd won a number of city and regional Science Olympiad awards, which were extremely prestigious in the Soviet Union at the time because the communist regime was nurturing a new generation of young scientists. The youngster also had a reputation as a difficult student after an incident in which his gym teacher had poked fun at him for being so poor at sports. He'd been so upset by this criticism that the boy had secretly smeared the teacher's whistle with caustic chemicals. This had made the teacher's lips and tongue turn black before swelling up and causing her speech to be slurred.

Detectives discovered that a few days before nutrition nurse Ekaterina Shcherban had been taken ill, she'd clashed with this same boy after catching him rummaging through the school refrigerator. So detectives focused their enquiries on the teenage pupil. They discovered that their prime suspect was abused and neglected but an extremely gifted child.

He frequently stole food and picked pockets at a nearby farmers' market because his violent, alcoholic mother did not feed him. She often banished her son from their home, so she could drink alcohol and take heroin with friends. As a result, kindly neighbours from the crumbling housing estate where the boy lived would feed him and often give him a bed for the night.

At first, police believed the boy's troubled background made him more likely to be the killer. He was hauled into a police station and interrogated with a view to getting a murder confession. During the grilling, the youth admitted sneaking into the school kitchen and stealing from the canteen refrigerator. He insisted he'd been starving hungry, having not eaten anything for the entire weekend before returning to school on Monday morning.

Officers raided the boy's home but turned up no trace of any poison, although they did uncover a lot of his mother's drug paraphernalia. The police also retraced the youth's recent footsteps to try and find out if he'd had contact with anyone who might have supplied the poison, but they failed to establish anything conclusive.

The boy did admit to having played that cruel prank on his gym teacher, which had ended with her suffering superficial burns to her mouth and lips. But he emphatically denied poisoning anyone. Detectives accused him of lying and remained convinced he was their school killer. Ivanyutina was delighted by the way the police had turned that student into their number one suspect. This enabled her to continue her revenge mission for what she believed was a conspiracy against her by the entire school.

One dogged young police detective pointed out to his colleagues that their chief suspect – the young pupil – had no clear motive for killing anyone, let alone all the students and staff members who'd so far either died or been taken seriously ill. The boy had never voiced hatred towards any of them.

It was only then that detectives discovered that chemistry teacher Natalya Kukarenko – who'd died – had a second job at the school: head of the canteen's food inventory. This meant she counted all food deliveries in and out of the school, and this had led to her and nurse Ekaterina Shcherban reprimanding Tamara Ivanyutina and banning her from taking any food home from the school.

* * *

A few days later, Tamara Ivanyutina strolled through the gates on her way into school when she came face to face with two police detectives at the entrance. They casually informed her that they were interviewing everyone connected to the school canteen. She was not in any way a suspect.

Ivanyutina's face darkened when the two officers explained why they were there. "I was outraged," she recalled. "How dare they come to me? I had nothing to hide. Those people all deserved what they got. I hadn't broken the law. In my mind it was justice. Pure and simple."

One of the detectives who encountered Ivanyutina that morning outside the school later said: "I was suspicious from the first moment I saw her looking at us. She seemed to instantly change character from being happy and whistling to herself into a dark, nasty woman when we mentioned the deaths at the school."

The investigators also noticed that Ivanyutina was not making any direct eye contact with them. Even more significantly, though, she seemed unwilling to show them around the school kitchen. "She behaved as if she owned the kitchen and we were insulting her by suggesting it might not be hygienic," one investigator recalled. And when the two detectives introduced Ivanyutina to a forensic scientist who'd just arrived to conduct an inspection of the kitchen, she shuddered with irritation.

Moments afterwards – as they approached the kitchen area – Ivanyutina stormed off in a huff, leaving the forensic scientist and detectives to examine the main kitchen area on their own. She walked into the side pantry that contained the main school refrigerator to find the school's assistant head teacher examining the fridge, which once again appeared to be faulty. He simply called the school handyman and it was fixed within minutes, much to Ivanyutina's annoyance.

Ivanyutina was so irritated to see that all the food had been salvaged that she failed to appreciate the significance of her negative reaction to those two detectives earlier. Instead, she removed an orange from a fruit bowl on the counter, took it into the toilet and injected it with thallium poison. Then she offered it to the assistant principal, who she knew liked to eat fresh fruit every day. He refused her offer of the orange, which left Ivanyutina fuming. Not once did she consider that he might be wary of accepting any gift from her because he already had suspicions about her involvement in the school deaths.

Ivanyutina convinced herself that if she made enough of a fuss they'd all stop searching her kitchen, give up and go home empty-handed. She simply didn't see what was on the horizon and believed she could bully them out of her kitchen. It was only then that the two detectives looked at each other wearily and realized properly, for the first time, that this grumpy woman was trying to hide something. It was made clear to Ivanyutina that she had no choice but to allow the police and forensics to carry out a detailed examination of the entire kitchen.

Ivanyutina was so immersed in her own world of murder and retribution that she didn't realize how guilty she was making herself look. In her mind, she'd simply dealt with her enemies and believed there was no way the police would think she was the killer. She was in a classically self-deluded state. As the forensic scientist and investigators began collecting samples from kitchen utensils and products, Ivanyutina tried to snatch some of them off the experts. She told them she needed to put them in a sink to be washed.

Ivanyutina's behaviour that morning convinced the investigators to take a closer look at her background. They quickly discovered that she'd hidden a criminal record when she'd applied for her job at the school. This wasn't unusual in the Soviet Union at the time, but the detectives heard rumours that Ivanyutina had provided sexual favours to the male schools official who'd signed off on her employment.

That evening, detectives knocked on the front door of the apartment on the outskirts of Kiev that Ivanyutina shared with her second husband. At first, she refused to let the officers in. Then one detective produced a search warrant, and she had no choice in the matter. Despite the sense that things were closing in on her, Ivanyutina stubbornly rejected all police accusations in her usual boorish manner as the investigators began searching the apartment.

Within a few minutes, forensic scientists and police officers noticed a small nightstand in the corner of Ivanyutina's bedroom. When they asked her about it, Ivanyutina looked nervous and mumbled that there was a sewing machine in it, which she'd inherited from her mother-in-law. The investigator assured Ivanyutina that he only needed to take a quick look but that he had to inspect it as part of his job.

Inside the nightstand, a bottle of engine oil was found, and one of the forensic examiners noticed that it seemed very heavy considering its contents. On closer inspection, the same expert immediately recognized the scent of the same notorious lethal poison called Clerici's solution, otherwise known as thallium, that had been found in the body of the dead chemistry teacher. Tamara Ivanyutina insisted that the strangely thick, brownish substance was household poison she'd used to tackle a pest problem. By admitting that she knew it was poison and that it belonged to her, Ivanyutina had pointed the finger of suspicion more firmly in her own direction.

The detectives deliberately switched subjects and disarmed Ivanyutina by confronting her about her secret criminal record. She dismissed suggestions that she'd given a school inspector sexual favours in exchange for him ignoring her criminal past. Ivanyutina calmly informed detectives that the best way to a successful life was to find a wealthy husband, not give sexual favours in exchange for a lowly school kitchen job. She candidly told detectives she'd walked away from the love of her life because he could not offer her financial security. Money was clearly important to her. Ivanyutina openly admitted to police that she'd made a few "bad investments" when she was trying to set up a business and that that was why she'd needed the job at the school.

Standing there, in her flat, she denied killing anyone, but by the time she arrived at the police station following the raid on her apartment, she'd clearly had a change of heart. During her preliminary interview, she suddenly announced to detectives that she believed that all her victims deserved to die so it didn't matter if she confessed everything to them. She claimed she'd had no choice but to kill and injure all those people at school number 16.

As she unravelled her crimes at the police station, she obsessively avoided mentioning her early life. One detective, believing it would hold some explanation for her actions, tried in various subtle ways to get her to talk about her own childhood, but she refused. Losing patience, the investigator eventually asked Ivanyutina outright: "Come on. Tell us about your family? What were they like?" She paused for a moment before speaking in a staccato voice that contained little or no emotion: "They taught me that you must punish your enemies before they punish you."

Within minutes it had become clear that Ivanyutina's childhood had helped turn her into a multiple killer.

* * *

Tamara Ivanyutina was born Tamara Maslenko in the city of Tula, 140 miles south of Moscow, in 1941. The Soviet Union's grim propiska accommodation system was in force at that time, which meant Ivanyutina's entire family shared one small apartment with others when she was growing up. Often as many as a dozen people would occupy the same rooms, with just one kitchen and one bathroom between them all. Each family – which could include up to three generations – had to somehow co-exist with others in that restricted living space.

Married couples often used flimsy screens to shield their beds from in-laws and children. But this could only happen if they had enough space in the first place. Rooms in these shared flats were so cramped that inhabitants slept on cots, side by side or at right angles to each other, often on the bare floor without mattresses.

Bathrooms were used at pre-agreed times of the day and night, according to strict schedules. On weekday mornings, the kitchen was jealously guarded and constantly fought over. Many residents ended up using chamber pots and cooking on camping stoves in their rooms. Fires happened with alarming regularity.

Rows and rows of laundry criss-crossed the kitchen and the bathtub most times of the day. The only sink in the flat was usually black from overuse and often cracked. There was the constant noise of people talking, arguing, having sex, screaming, crying, listening to the radio, all confined in one tiny space. The walls and ceilings of these apartments were usually mouldy from dampness and condensation caused by the overcrowding. One former resident later described each flat as "a slum within a slum".

And in the centre of all this were Ivanyutina's parents Anton and Maria Maslenko, who'd long since smashed the emotional bridge between right and wrong to pieces thanks to their heavy consumption of alcohol and inbuilt paranoia. Life in the Maslenkos' communal propiska home revolved around frequent skirmishes with fellow residents. Ivanyutina's parents never complained to the authorities because, in Soviet Russia back then, that would get them labelled as troublemakers, which meant being sent to the back of queues for everything from food to a new home. It was better to sort out any disputes personally. To many who knew them back then, the Maslenkos seemed a very solitary family. None of them ever smiled. They tended to put their heads down and walk on without saying a word when others were around.

Today, psychiatrists believe that this kind of overcrowding can often, ironically, lead to a feeling of isolation combined with a complete inability to measure and control one's reaction to any problems. Whenever things got too difficult for the Maslenkos in that community apartment, they started to take the law into their own hands.

Little Tamara Ivanyutina knew nothing about all this during the war years when she was very young. With German bombs dropping all over the city on a regular basis, her family's main priority would have been to survive in one piece. She admitted that her earliest memories revolved around a chilling combination of air raids and furious rows between her parents and their neighbours. At that time, Ivanyutina was a very shy, withdrawn little girl, clearly afraid of saying anything out of turn in case it angered her stern but drunken parents.

Over the first eight to ten years of Ivanyutina's life, the Maslenkos moved home regularly, swapping one bombed-out *propiska* for another in a city that had struggled in the aftermath of the Second World War, which had left Russia broken after their hard-won victory over the Germans. But no matter how many times the Maslenkos changed homes, they still managed to upset their neighbours.

More than five decades after this, Ivanyutina was asked by detectives how she came to use that lethal thallium poison at the school where she worked.

Straight-faced and without any emotion, Ivanyutina informed detectives that she'd first come across the poison through her own parents. They'd used it ever since the 1930s when, she claimed, her father had poisoned a neighbour during a dispute.

Anton Maslenko later admitted using the thallium as an "act of retaliation" against that neighbour because of his pro-Soviet beliefs, which had irritated the Maslenko couple immensely. From that moment on, Ivanyutina's mother Maria had always kept a container of thallium poison in the family home. The Maslenkos knew only too well that it could cause severe cardiac inactivity, joint pain, insomnia, vitamin deficiency and kidney problems – and often death.

One middle-aged neighbour who lived next the family in Tula ended up being rushed to hospital with excruciating abdominal and joint pain, as well as a burning sensation in her feet and calves. Soon after admission, she also began losing her hair. A few days afterwards, she died from what doctors said was a cardiac arrest, although doctors later conceded that they had been puzzled by her unusual symptoms. Shortly after this, another resident who shared a *propiska* apartment with the Maslenkos was murdered by them after making a nasty remark about how Maria hadn't cleaned the toilet properly.

By this time, Ivanyutin – aged 10 – was openly sympathizing with her parents' actions. She later recalled that there had been plenty of children at her school whom she would dearly have loved to dispose of. But she left all the killings to her mother and father when she was a child. Psychiatrists said she was most likely preparing herself, in a sense, to commit similar crimes one day.

Whenever Ivanyutina discovered that her parents had poisoned neighbours, she ignored it because she wanted to ensure they loved her as much as they seemed to love her prettier, older sister Nina.

While still living in Tula, four of Ivanyutina's siblings left home after stumbling on evidence of their parents' murderous habits. The three sons and daughter who walked out said they had to leave as they were afraid of being implicated in their family's killings.

Anton and Maria Maslenko and daughters Nina and Tamara eventually moved to Kiev. Ivanyutina was not yet in her twenties, but she soon made herself popular with local young men, some of whom claimed she was very "easy" when it came to sexual relationships. Ivanyutina blamed her promiscuity on feeling like an outsider in comparison to most of the young people she met in Kiev. They'd all seemed so much more sophisticated than her. She recalled: "I wanted them to like me, so I gave the men what they wanted but they still loathed me anyway."

Her mother and father had always blamed communism for the poverty-stricken life they'd been forced to live. Anton Maslenko believed that he and his family had – along with millions of others – been forced to move to the big cities for work as part of Stalin's policies, which had devastated that region of the Soviet Union in the early 1930s.

Anton regularly told all his children that they should never trust mankind and should take anything that was offered because no one would help them. He insisted that this attitude would be the key to their survival. Ivanyutina's parents also made it doubly clear to the two daughters who'd stayed with them that they must escape their ghetto life as soon as they were old enough. They told them to make sure they found money and comfort whatever it took.

When Ivanyutina was in her early twenties, her mother Maria was rushed to a Kiev hospital following a heart attack. Tamara initially wondered if her mother's ill health had been caused by poison administered by her father but soon dismissed such notions when she saw how heartbroken he was.

While Anton Maslenko was visiting his sickly wife in hospital, one of her relatives turned up at the bedside and announced coldly that she didn't expect Maria to recover from her illness. Anton Maslenko was crestfallen by what his wife's relative was saying as he genuinely could not contemplate life without her. The same woman further compounded the situation by talking about funeral plans for Maria as if she was already dead.

It was only afterwards that it dawned on Mr Maslenko that his wife's female relative had been suggesting that they start a relationship behind Maria's back as she lay dying in hospital. He was appalled.

Maria eventually made a full recovery, but Anton Maslenko couldn't get the words of that woman out of his head. A few weeks later, the same woman visited Maria at home and Anton offered her a drink of local moonshine. The woman knocked it back in one gulp, unaware that Anton had put some thallium drops in it. Then he proposed a toast to his wife's good health and – in accordance with Russian tradition – the two ate some finger foods with their vodka. Within a few days, the woman was dead.

Anton Maslenko attended his victim's funeral with his wife, who was extremely relieved that he'd never been tempted by that woman's attempt at seduction. Mr Maslenko later admitted: "That woman dared to imagine the death of my beloved Maria Fyodorovna. She had no right to do that."

Shortly after this, Maria turned up on another neighbour's doorstep with fritters laced with thallium as "a peace offering" after the two had fallen out. The neighbour decided not to eat the fritters and gave them to her cat instead. That night she watched the pet die in agony and was in no doubt that those fritters had been poisoned. The neighbour's life had been saved by a combination of her own suspicious nature and the fact that she'd heard rumours about the Maslenkos' poisoning of other neighbours. Others were less lucky.

Another victim was an elderly disabled Second World War veteran, whose only "offence" was to be receiving generous veterans' benefits, which Mr and Mrs Maslenko were extremely jealous about. They considered this very unfair, so Maria responded by presenting the old soldier with a stack of pancakes sprinkled with thallium. He died soon afterwards.

By the early 1970s, Ivanyutina's parents Anton and Maria were living in a rundown apartment in a leaking mansion in the crumbling centre of Kiev. It was a nineteenth-century neo-Gothic structure known as the Lone Knight's House. By this time, the once-impressive building had rotting staircases, sagging floors and wooden latticework peeking through disintegrating plaster. It had been worn out by decades of *propiska*-type overcrowding and a lack of maintenance, and a fire had damaged the structure of the building some years earlier.

Soon Mr and Mrs Maslenko were embroiled in yet another bitter conflict with a fellow resident. This one had dared to turn the volume up on his television set. The couple became so infuriated by the man's refusal to turn it down that they eventually killed him with a fresh supply of their favourite poison, this time obtained by Ivanyutina's older sister Nina. She'd got it through a friend who was an employee of the Geological Institute, based in nearby Minsk. Geologists used thallium to determine the density of minerals. Not long after this, another neighbour made a disparaging remark to the Maslenkos about their hygiene. Within days, that neighbour was also dead.

Ivanyutina told detectives following her arrest for the school number 16 murders that her sister Nina had got more thallium from her friend in order to murder her husband just a few days after their wedding. He left her a very comfortable private apartment in the centre of Kiev.

Nina soon found herself another, wealthier, lover. He refused to marry her, though, and had the temerity to suggest to Nina they live together "in sin" and forget about marriage altogether. Nina was so upset by this that a few days later she put some drops of thallium poison in her new lover's borscht. It wasn't enough to kill him, but it did make him very sick and rendered him impotent. Tamara Ivanyutina later claimed that this had been Nina's way of telling her boyfriend she had expected him to marry her.

Ivanyutina herself resembled a bulky local milkmaid, who smelt of stale, home-cooked meals and disinfectant. One relative described her as the type of woman Russians would refer to as "visible" (the English translation would be "striking".) Despite this, she believed that by giving the clear impression of being someone who could be a source of domestic comfort and protection, she'd soon find a needy husband, which is precisely what eventually happened.

He turned out to be a hard-working trucker. Ivanyutina had been impressed as he made good money and had his own two-room apartment in Kiev.

However – allegedly encouraged by her mother Maria and sister Nina – Ivanyutina decided to poison her first husband just a few days after their marriage using thallium, which she went on to give to all those pupils and staff at school number 16.

Ivanyutina first tested it out on a neighbour's cats and chickens in order to calculate what dosage would be required to ensure her new husband died.

She added thallium to her husband's food, believing it would accumulate in his body and gradually kill him in such a way that no one would be suspicious about why he had died.

Ivanyutina's first husband quickly experienced severe weakness and pain in his legs and his hair began to fall out. But he insisted on continuing to work as a truck driver, despite his illness. He even persuaded Ivanyutina to accompany him on a long road trip across Russia. As she sat next to him in the cab of the truck, she watched his every move avidly in case there were any further tell-tale signs of the poison. If that happened, she would need to force him to stop the lorry to avoid being hurt or killed in a crash.

Halfway through the journey of more than a thousand miles across the centre of Russia, Ivanyutina's husband said that he could barely feel the pedals due to the numbness in his legs and that he needed to stop the truck. Moments later, he slammed his foot on the brake so erratically that the lorry almost tipped over as it slewed to a halt on the side of an icy road. He begged Ivanyutina to get behind the wheel so they could complete the journey and he could earn some much-needed cash.

With Ivanyutina now behind the wheel, they eventually stopped at an isolated truck park next to a river with the express intention of sleeping in the bed at the back of the cab. Ivanyutina later admitted not having given much thought to the fact that her husband was dying in front of her very eyes from the poison she'd fed to him. As she recalled: "My main concern was that we completed the driving job, so he got paid because I wanted the money."

The following morning, before sunrise, Ivanyutina sat in the cab of the lorry with the headlights on full beam as her weak and exhausted husband tried to bring himself to life by bathing in a freezing cold river. She told detectives straight-faced following her arrest for the school killings that she hadn't wanted him to die just yet.

After stumbling out of the river, her husband dried his head with a towel, only to find it covered with his hair, which had come out in clumps. Ivanyutina eventually got out of the cab of the truck and helped her husband get dressed, determined to keep him alive long enough to get the money he was due for that driving job.

The following day they returned to their apartment. Her husband collapsed almost immediately and was rushed to hospital. None of the doctors at the hospital realized he was the victim of poisoning. And when he died two days later, they insisted he'd been killed by a massive heart attack.

Years afterwards, Ivanyutina was asked by one detective during her interrogation if she felt it was ironic that, having poisoned her first husband, she had had to risk her own life by accompanying him on that last fateful driving job. The detective recalled: "Tamara turned and glared at me. 'What do you mean ironic?'. She clearly had no idea what the word meant."

Then, after at least a minute's silence, Ivanyutina shrugged her shoulders and told the detective: "Don't you understand? I had to be in that lorry to make sure he got paid. I wanted the money." As the same investigator recalled: "That's when I realized she was the coldest person I have ever met in my life. She was so focused on the money that she was quite prepared to do anything to make sure he completed that last driving job."

Following Ivanyutina's husband's death, she sold the flat they'd shared and moved to the centre of Kiev, where she met a man called Oleg Ivanyutin. "She made it all sound like a business transaction as she told us this," one of the detectives who interviewed her recalled. "Then I asked her about Oleg's family and she looked me right in the eye before admitting almost proudly that they hated her guts."

Ivanyutin told the detectives during that interview that her new boyfriend Oleg did not have his own apartment but lived with his elderly parents, who also owned a second home in the Krasnodar district of Kiev. Oleg's mother and father had loathed Ivanyutina on sight. She was seven years older than their son, and they wondered if the couple would ever provide them with some grandchildren.

Their wedding went ahead in the summer of 1983. Ivanyutina and Oleg immediately moved into the parents' spare property and sold it quickly. Then they purchased a new home, near the centre of Kiev and close to where her parents lived. She liked the house so much that she set up a small farm in the yard and hoped to make a good income from it.

Oleg's parents had upset her immensely. She hated their attitude towards her so decided it was time to show them why they were wrong. She particularly loathed Oleg's father for daring to pressurize her and her new husband to have children, when nothing could have been further from her mind. She'd made a pledge to herself never to have children after what she'd been through as a child.

The "child issue" between Oleg, Ivanyutina and his parents dominated the early days and months of their marriage. Mr and Mrs Ivanyutin gave the couple an ultimatum: either they produced a child within a year, or the Ivanyutin's would change their will and bequeath the valuable house they lived in to someone else. Ivanyutina was outraged by their plan, which she saw as a direct threat to her financial stability, something she'd strived to achieve all her adult life after a childhood of dire poverty and unhappiness.

After yet another uncomfortable conversation with her husband's parents, Oleg's pensioner father – who'd always been a relatively healthy person – suddenly began to suffer from severe pain in his legs and numbness of his feet. Within days he was hospitalized. Doctors diagnosed an exacerbation of polyarthritis, prescribed a drug treatment and sent him home.

Ivanyutina was irritated that she clearly hadn't administered enough poison in his food a few days earlier. So she pretended to be so worried about her father-in-law's health that she persuaded her husband to take a trip to his family home to see how he was. Within minutes of the couple arriving at the house, Ivanyutina found herself alone in her in-laws' kitchen and carefully administered some drops of thallium poison into a bowl of soup which was about to be taken up on a tray to her bedridden father-in-law. Ivanyutina – sitting alongside her husband – watched closely as her father-in-law demolished the soup in next to no time, even reluctantly complimenting her cooking.

A few hours later – as Ivanyutina and Oleg drove back from her in-laws' home – his father collapsed and was rushed by ambulance back to the same hospital he'd been discharged from a few days earlier. He died in agony the following morning, but none of the doctors who examined him believed there was anything suspicious about his death.

Each time Ivanyutina finished yet another chilling aspect of her life story while being interrogated by detectives following her arrest for the school poisonings, they presumed she'd reached the end of her confessions.

"Then she'd pause for a few moments," one officer recalled, "Catch her breath and move onto something that was usually more shocking than the previous story." For Tamara Ivanyutina had had plenty more "work" to do following the killing of her father-in-law.

She revealed to detectives how his funeral was an understandably solemn affair, which involved a pedestrian procession, with the casket on an antique horse-drawn carriage as the mourners wound slowly through the streets towards the cemetery. Behind them all was an orchestra blaring a few bars of Chopin's funeral march, as those attending scattered a trail of carnations and pine branches on the tarmac.

While her heartbroken husband Oleg looked down at the ground most of the time, Ivanyutina held her head up high and panned the crowd for onlookers with an expression of pride and determination on her face. One who attended the funeral of Oleg's father recalled: "I remember watching Ivanyutina. She looked as if she didn't have a care in the world. As the music got louder while we walked along the street to the church, she hummed along to it in a relaxed manner and you could see she was pleased about something."

Husband Oleg told police after his wife's arrest that it felt as if she was happy to see the suffering of others. When Oleg remarked on her upbeat demeanour, she replied pithily: "It is not the dead one should fear, but the living."

As the mourners at Oleg's father's funeral bade farewell following a solemn wake at the family home, Ivanyutina's mother-in-law complained of feeling ill and at one stage clutched her heart. Ivanyutina described during her interview with police how she offered sympathy and promised to get a painkiller from the bathroom to help ease the pain.

Moments later she slipped a small phial out of her handbag and poured the contents into a glass before handing it to her mother-in-law.

Within minutes, Oleg's elderly mother was suffering from severe nausea and blurred vision. When she tried to get up from her chair, she felt so dizzy that she slumped back down on the seat. Then she glared across the room at Ivanyutina, who glanced back at her with a complete look of indifference. "She's poisoned me," screamed Ivanyutina's mother-in-law. "That evil woman has done this."

Instead of looking shocked, Ivanyutin smiled as she stared defiantly at the old lady. One of the other mourners recalled: "Tamara kept her eyes on the widow for what seemed like ages. The rest of us tried to look away and ignore what had been said." Ivanyutina admitted to detectives during her police station interview that she'd wanted her mother-in-law to know what she'd done and wanted her to die a horrible death.

When her struggling mother-in-law repeated the same allegation, Ivanyutina exploded into a rage and branded her mother-in-law a liar who'd always disapproved of her being her son's wife. With other mourners looking aghast at her outburst, Oleg stepped forward and defended his wife. Moments later, she "accidently" dropped the phial containing the remains of the "medicine" on the hardwood floor. It smashed into pieces. Some of those present at the wake that day said they had no doubt she'd done that deliberately.

Following her father-in-law's funeral, Ivanyutina went to bed in a very good mood, she told detectives. But when she demanded sex from her husband, she couldn't understand why he was too upset about his mother and father to perform. Instead of being sympathetic to Oleg, Ivanyutina sulked after not getting what she wanted. As she lay in bed next to her grieving husband that night, she decided that his rejection of her was the ultimate insult.

A few days later, Oleg's mother died in hospital after suffering almost identical symptoms to her late husband. Doctors said she'd died from heart problems. It was then that Ivanyutina began the process that she hoped would lead to her second husband's death. But first she bought more pigs and hens for their new business and convinced him they'd one day make a good living.

* * *

Ivanyutina unravelled all these extraordinary details to her interrogators in the police station following her arrest for the school number 16 poisonings. Her 24-hour-long confession left investigators bewildered and drained. One of the officers present that day recalled: "At one stage she referred to her victims as rats, who'd upset her and had had to be exterminated in exactly the same way her own parents had dealt with troublesome neighbours."

Ivanyutina tried to convince detectives that the poisoning of many of the pupils at school number 16 had been an accident and that she hadn't meant to hurt them, let alone kill some of them. When officers pointed out to her that she'd had a lot of experience using thallium poison before all this, she ignored them.

In the end, Ivanyutina's extraordinary confession about her and her family's use of thallium convinced detectives to order the exhumation of the bodies of her in-laws, so that toxicology examinations could be carried out.

Detectives found out that Ivanyutina's current husband Oleg had been rushed to hospital critically ill just two days earlier. When investigators visited Oleg to try and interview him about his wife, they immediately noticed that all his hair had fallen out, which was one of the symptoms suffered by many of the school poisoning victims. Oleg was on his last legs due to genuine ill health after a stroke. His wife hadn't had a chance to poison him yet.

Doctors at the hospital warned detectives that Oleg was unlikely to survive. He wasn't able to sit up in bed and could barely talk. Detectives assured Oleg that Ivanyutina would have targeted him eventually, so he needed to help them bring her to justice. Initially, Oleg refused to believe the detective's allegations against Ivanyutina. So the following day, investigators returned to his hospital bedside with the toxicology report detailing the causes of his parents' deaths. Oleg still refused to accept that his wife was a mass murderer. He insisted Ivanyutina simply had a "strange obsession" with funerals. Oleg said that Ivanyutina was entranced by the malevolent, sentient atmosphere that accompanied all funeral processions. None of it made any logical sense. As the detectives pointed out: Why would anyone kill people just in order to go to their funerals?

Back at the police station, detectives, now armed with Ivanyutina's full written confession, handed the case over to prosecutors, who considered it a foregone conclusion that Ivanyutina would be convicted at her coming trial.

Believing that her sister Nina had been instrumental in supplying the poison, the detectives examined her role more closely, although she was a much less cut-and-dried suspect. Nina was eventually charged with and convicted of just one murder, but there was a suspicion that Ivanyutina may have pointed the finger at her just because she was jealous of her good looks and the fact she was her parents' favourite child.

The allegation that Nina had supplied the entire family with thallium poison at various times was played down by prosecutors at the time, to the surprise of many. Rumours emerged that Nina may have given evidence against her sister and parents in exchange for a lenient sentence. There was also the woman geology laboratory technician who had supplied Nina with the thallium in the first place to contend with. She was never charged with any offence and managed to keep her name out of the media during coverage of the case, and remains a mystery to this day.

Ivanyutina remained defiant and convinced of her innocence throughout her own trial, showing no hint of remorse, which did seem to fit the personality traits exposed by her catalogue of chilling crimes. When the chief judge asked Ivanyutina at the very end of the hearing if she wished to apologize to her victims, she replied that she wasn't the apologizing kind.

That response was the very last thing Ivanyutina ever said in public. In late 1986, she was found guilty of 20 poisoning cases, 9 of which were fatal, and was sentenced to death.

Throughout Ivanyutina's well-publicized trial, the phrase "serial killer" was never directly used. Instead she was described as a "maniac killer". Authorities were determined not to use phrases that would draw a comparison between the Soviet Union and the decadent West.

Ivanyutina was stunned on hearing the execution announcement by the judge and refused to react to it. One detective who interrogated her following her arrest recalled: "I don't think she'd ever considered that she would be actually executed. She never referred to it and always sounded as if she was expecting to be released from prison at any moment. She was in a state of complete and utter denial."

Ivanyutina's father Anton and mother Maria faced a separate trial for the murder of Maria's relative, who'd made that suggestive comment when Maria had been sick in hospital back in Tula. Her parents were eventually found guilty and received 13 and 10 years of imprisonment respectively. Neither of them lived long enough to be released from prison.

Their other daughter Nina was sentenced to 16 years for causing the death of a neighbour of her parents by providing the poison used to commit the murder. She ended up serving 15 years, and her sister's allegation that Nina had murdered her very elderly husband was never the subject of criminal charges. Nina disappeared immediately after her release from prison.

Following the trials of the Maslenko family members, investigators described the parents and their two daughters as being arrogant and resentful. They also said they were over-sensitive to perceived slights and had an inflated opinion of themselves. Following the convictions, police claimed that a total of 40 people had most likely been poisoned by Maslenko family members, and that 13 of those victims had died.

In prison, Ivanyutina continued to deny she'd done anything wrong, despite having admitted to the murders. She insisted she did not deserve to be punished, let alone sentenced to death. Not long after her sentencing, she offered a clumsy bribe to a Kiev police officer to enable her to be released from prison by promising him "a lot of gold". Another detective recalled: "That was typical of Tamara. She never took responsibility for her actions but she believed it was her god-given right to be released from prison and have her death sentence commuted."

Fresh public demands that dozens more murders linked to the family should be investigated were ignored by officials, who admitted that authorities in Kiev couldn't afford the cost of relaunching another mass murder investigation into a family that had already confessed to multiple killings.

In the late autumn of 1987, Ivanyutina became the third and last woman in the USSR sentenced to death after the end of the Second World War. As seemed to be the way, she was shot dead with a single bullet in the back of the head at the Lukyanivska detention centre in Kiev, where she'd been incarcerated since her trial. The exact date of her actual execution was kept secret by authorities in accordance with Soviet practices at that time. The case was considered deeply embarrassing to the nation. It is not known to this day how her body was disposed of.

A notification of her death was sent to her sister Nina and her other siblings, who'd walked out on the family after those earlier killings committed by their parents. There was no memorial service held for her.

Ivanyutina once said of her troubled childhood that she'd never forgotten the look of complete and utter satisfaction on her parents' faces after they'd "disposed" of one troublesome neighbour. She recalled that her mother's mood always lifted after she'd killed someone who annoyed her.

CHAPTER THREE

THE IMPRINTING ANIMAL

Schepkinsky Forest, north-east Rostov,
Russia, 21 December 1978

The brutality of a city's past can irretrievably damage the personalities and character traits of its current citizens. In the case of Rostov, the city suffered enormous pain and anguish, like so many Soviet cities bombarded by the Germans during the Second World War, but particularly during the battle for the city in 1941.

No one, it seems, was exempt from the senseless violence inflicted on Rostov back then, not even the innocent patients of the city's only psychiatric clinic. Just days after the Germans invaded, they were ordered into sealed vans and gassed. The Nazis also set up a POW camp for troublesome locals within the city boundaries. The loved ones of many citizens were dragged there and never seen again. Some inmates were forced to help German soldiers round up the city's Jewish population in preparation for their large-scale annihilation. Others were given guns and encouraged to go out onto the city streets and shoot Jews in exchange for their own freedom.

The word "Rostrov" means "growth" in Russian, and following the city's appalling experiences during the Second World War, most citizens were determined to re-invent the city and turn it back into the thriving metropolis it had once been. Vast swathes of discarded wasteground on the edge of the city were turned into parks and forests to try and lift the spirits of the population following all their suffering at the hands of the Germans. These forestry reserves were known as *zakarniks* in Russian. Normally hard-faced communist party officials recognized that citizens needed an opportunity to enjoy a proper outdoor lifestyle.

One of those newly developed recreation areas was Schepkinsky Forest, on the north-east edge of Rostov. It was one of the biggest woodland plantations ever created in the whole of the Soviet Union at that time and was designated as an area of great natural beauty. It was named after the Schepkinskaya Gully, a huge bowl of reservoir water at the northern end of the forest.

Rostrov authorities converted an abandoned quarry inside Schepkinsky Forest into a lake, where people were encouraged to swim. It was filled with Prussian carp, crayfish and monkey goby. Fishing licences were not required in a bid to encourage visitors. A pond was also created in the centre of the forest, although bathing was prohibited due to large pike and poison-ous water snakes. To the east of the forest, there was luscious marshland formed by the tributaries of the Bolshaya Kamy-shevakha and Temernik rivers.

The natural inhabitants of Schepkinsky Forest included Roe deer, foxes, hares, wild boars, pheasants, partridges, herons and at least two species of bear, all of which thrived thanks to a hunting ban put in place to improve the area's ecological foot-print. And on the edge of this brand new, sprawling beauty spot lay the small village of Schepkino, which contained the only community for many miles around.

The forest proved a great success until the late 1960s, when there were a number of attacks on people by wild animals. At the time, three unruly bears killed a young couple, so this *zakaznik* began to be abandoned by Rostov's needy citizens. It earned itself a new nickname, "the ghost forest", as people were too afraid to enter it. Forest rangers were phased out after local government financial cuts, so there would often be no one in there.

The villagers of nearby Schepkino recalled increasingly eery noises coming from the forest, especially at night. They presumed these were the sounds of that vast array of wild creatures roaming freely, who often clashed with each other under cover of darkness. But the noises coming from the centre of the forest late on the evening of 21 December 1978 were worse than anything the villagers had ever heard before

– ear-piercing screams followed by the sound of rustling through the thick undergrowth.

In the pitch black forest that night a wild animal had bared its teeth before feasting on its prey, a prey that was now crumpled up on the winter moss under the moonlit shade of a huge oak tree. Each time he took another mouthful, he noisily squelched, crunched and sucked to make the meat easier to swallow. He particularly enjoyed consuming the tongue of his victims.

Afterwards, he stood over the remains proudly before finally slashing maniacally at them once again with a knife. The excitement of the kill had turned this normally mellow creature into a wild beast with no self-control, just an incredible urge to satisfy a desire to taste and devour fresh meat. This is what psychologists call "imprinting", when a creature develops an insatiable appetite for killing in such a way that it can never again be suppressed.

No doubt most of the other wild animals of the forest must have given a collective sigh of relief that evening as the beast departed at speed through the thick, prickly foliage, brushing clumps of greenery out of the way while heading southwards to where he'd entered the forest just a few hours earlier. He eventually burst out onto a narrow, muddy track that led towards the village. His heavy breathing had calmed since the attack. He stopped for a moment to make sure there was no one around before continuing his journey.

The beast had never killed like this before. Now he had crossed the line for the first time, and this would unleash a catalogue of death and destruction.

* * *

The bloodied remains of that attack were spotted from a distance by a rare walker in Schepkinsky Forest at daybreak the following morning. He alerted the police and advised them to take the remains away before any other wild animals began feeding on it.

The first patrolmen to arrive at the scene drew their revolvers as they moved tentatively through the foliage, in case any of the wild animals were still in the vicinity. As the scattered remains came closer into view, one of the two officers noticed what appeared to be a human head. He immediately stopped, turned and vomited on the ground. He and his colleague had noticed two human arms attached to two small hands.

Both policemen presumed a child must have been killed by a wild bear. They glanced down again at the head facing upwards just a few feet away. There were neat, empty sockets where the eyes should have been as opposed to what would have been left if a bird had pecked them out. One eyeball could be seen on the ground near to the corpse, untouched. The other one was never recovered. It was only then that it dawned on the two police officers that this child might have been killed by another person. The victim's name was Lena Zakotnova and she was just nine years old.

Where did all this pent-up rage come from in the first place? How could a human being devour an innocent child like this? To find out, one has to first step back into the Soviet Union's troubled and brutal past, which peaked so catastrophically in the middle of the twentieth century.

* * *

Andrei Chikatilo was born on 16 October 1936 in the Ukrainian village of Yablochnoye, then part of the USSR. Leader Joseph Stalin ruled the Soviet Union with an iron fist at that time. He'd ordered that all crops produced in the region should be collected and distributed to the rest of Russia. Chikatilo was born just three years after the mass famine caused by this. Almost four million citizens are said to have died in Ukraine because they had no food to eat at that time.

Stalin had also insisted that Ukraine's smaller independent farms should be replaced with state-run operations. Those who refused to give up their land were shot and killed, and anyone caught hiding grain from Stalin's crop collectors was sent to prison. Out of desperation, many of the peasants began eating dogs, cats, tree bark and roots. Others turned to cannibalism in order to survive.

This period is known by many in the region as "Holodomor", which combines the Ukrainian words for "starvation" with "to inflict death". It undoubtedly left a lifelong imprint on the lives of those who survived, as well as their relatives.

As a child, Andrei Chikatilo suffered from severe near-sightedness, along with lesions and water in his brain, most likely caused by the Holodomor. His home was a one-room hut shared with his parents and, eventually, a sister. His mother and father were both farm workers, who'd constantly struggled financially due to the famine. Andrei slept in the same bed as his parents. These close sleeping conditions led to violence and humiliation after Andrei wet the bed, which was an unfortunate side effect of his ailments.

Every time he had an "accident", his mother, Anna, would beat him as punishment. Andrei Chikatilo also had to deal with being told by his mother when he was just four or five years old that he'd had an older brother called Stepan, who'd been taken by neighbours and eaten before Andrei was born during the famine.

Chikatilo later claimed that this revelation about his brother had a profound effect on him. Experts believe that he most likely suffered a form of post-traumatic stress after hearing what had happened and it undoubtedly affected him for the rest of his life.

During the early stages of the Second World War, Chikatilo's father, Roman, was drafted to fight for the motherland against the Germans. The boy, then aged four or five, didn't see him again for years. In his home town of Yablochnoye,

Chikatilo lived through the brutal effects of the Nazis' Blitz-krieg, during which bombs rained down on the city almost every week. One bomb hit the family's flimsy hut just after he and his mother had managed to scramble into a nearby field. They watched as their home burnt to the ground. Shortly after this, Chikatilo's baby sister Tatyana was born. No one in the family ever satisfactorily explained who'd impregnated his mother, and there were rumours in the neighbourhood that she'd been raped by a German soldier.

It wasn't until 1948 – three years after the end of the war – that Chikatilo's father arrived home. It turned out he'd been captured and imprisoned by the Germans. But what should have been a joyous occasion for his young son and the rest of his family was tainted with doubt. Other citizens – many of whom had lost relatives in the war – cruelly ridiculed Chikatilo's father and labelled him a traitor after he survived the war, unlike so many millions of other Russians.

The humiliation of Chikatilo's father by the town had a serious knock-on effect on his young son. At school, pupils accused the boy of being "a coward's son", which made him the inevitable focus of school bullying. He became more introverted and ventured outside his home less and less, apart from to attend school. Chikatilo's father was by this time either ignored or spat on in the streets near their home for not having given his life for the motherland during the war. The same local children also confronted the young boy about his younger sister, whom everyone knew had been born in the middle of the war when his father was away fighting. They called her the "German bitch" and accused Chikatilo and his family of being Nazis.

And there was another knock-on effect caused by this hatred and innuendo. When Andrei Chikatilo reached his early teens, he was humiliated on a number of occasions when his attempt at adolescent romance failed miserably. There were rumours that he was not able to kiss girls, let alone perform sexually. The gossip in his village was that he was gay, although he fiercely denied it.

Aged 15, he tried to have sex with a girl to prove his "masculinity" but ended up ejaculating immediately and was ridiculed by his contemporaries after they heard what had happened from the girl in question. Later, he told all this to a psychiatrist and admitted that his experiences had left him angry and bewildered by his own reaction to girls.

Before leaving school, Andrei Chikatilo applied to go to university, where he hoped to get a law degree. But he failed the entry exam. He then did national service for two years before, in 1960, moving to Rodionovo-Nesvetayevsky – a town near the region's capital, Rostov – where he became a telephone engineer.

In 1963 – aged 26 – he married a woman called Feodosia "Fayina" Odnacheva two weeks after meeting her on a blind date arranged by his younger sister Tatyana. He and his wife had two children: first, a daughter, Lyudmila – born either 1964 or 1965 – followed by a younger son, Yuri, born in 1969. Both were conceived when Chikalito masturbated and inseminated his wife with his semen manually, as he was unable to maintain an erection while having intercourse, likely a repercussion of his earlier embarrassing experiences with sex.

Having a family at least enabled Chikatilo to lead what he thought was a "normal life" throughout most of the 1960s. At the end of that decade, he re-applied to university and was accepted to study Russian Literature at the Rostov Liberal Arts University. In 1972, he received a degree and immediately found a job as a teacher. But he was quickly forced to resign from that job after the parents of one of his pupils complained that he had tried to sexually assault their son. Chikatilo's emphatic denial was accepted by the school, but it was agreed that he should leave his job anyway. However, he managed to get another teaching post shortly after. He was soon under investigation for a similar offence at that job, too. A string of complaints about indecent assaults on children would force him to move from school to school, before he finally settled at a mining school in Shakhty, on the outskirts of Rostov.

Chikatilo later claimed he got little or no respect from his pupils or fellow staff at that school, or any of the other ones where he'd previously taught, as he was considered "weird" and "shy". From reports, some staff at those schools were aware of those previous incidents, yet he was still allowed to continue teaching. But did the unpleasant and suspicious treatment he suffered at the time make him scared of his own students? He didn't seem able to gain their respect and, as a result, often struggled to control his classroom. This made Chikalito resentful towards his pupils, and he later cited this as a reason why he molested some of them. He insisted it was the only way he could get any of them to respect him.

Not surprisingly, Chikatilo was forced out of the teaching profession after 10 years. Yet he was never actually arrested or prosecuted for molesting students. The Soviet education system at that time preferred to remove sexual predators from their jobs rather than put them in jail and admit to the world that such problems existed in their proud but damaged nation.

A job as a clerk in a raw materials factory in Rostov soon followed his final dismissal from teaching. This meant he had to travel by bus and train to work due to its long distance from the home he shared with his wife and two children.

Despite the previous accusations against him from all those schools, Chikatilo continued to be considered by friends and family as a good father and husband and a loyal member of the communist party. But this was all a facade; he later admitted he'd grown frustrated and angry due to his own impotence and sexual confusion. He was secretly trying to come to terms with being gay, but he didn't know how to deal with it himself, let alone tell his wife. Chikatilo later recalled that in order to combat the feeling that he might be gay, he'd convinced himself that he needed to find females prepared to have sex with him so he could prove to himself that he wasn't gay.

The other toxic emotional force driving Chikatilo on was that he continued to be haunted by what had happened to his brother. He once said that he constantly wondered why, if his parents had eaten his brother, they hadn't eaten him too? He claimed he had regular nightmares about his brother, during which he watched as his parents feasted on the boy's remains.

Chikatilo started immersing himself in a self-perpetuating fantasy world that revolved around forcing women to have sex before eating them. He didn't act out his fantasies but later admitted daydreaming about them constantly. Inevitably, he began studying more and more young people out on the streets on Rostov and wondering if they would help him turn his fantasies into reality.

At the same time, he wanted to go back to teaching, which he knew was a lot better for his head than working in a factory. He later claimed that a lot of his fantasies were fuelled by the boredom of his mundane job. He also had to face the reality that he would never work as a teacher again because all his applications for teaching jobs were turned down once his references were checked out.

Chikatilo began carrying a briefcase around with him at all times, which at least made him feel as if he was still a teacher. Sometimes he'd chat to complete strangers at the bus and train stations that he used to travel to and from his factory job. He'd tell those he talked to that he was still a teacher, and he liked the way most of them immediately trusted him more. He later admitted having relished the feeling of superiority and power, since he knew the truth about himself and they didn't. Initially, he remained happy enough chatting to strangers without taking his fantasies to another level.

On 21 December 1978, Chikatilo found himself in a Rostov railway station and spotted nine-year-old Lena Zakotnova sitting on her own on an empty bench after her mother went into a café to buy some food. By the time the mother had returned a few minutes later, Lena had disappeared. A few hours afterwards, Chikatilo emerged from Schepkinsky Forest with that little schoolgirl's blood literally on his hands.

Police who arrived at the railway station to investigate the child's disappearance that same evening were given a description of Chikatilo by a young student who'd been given a business card by the middle-aged former teacher just minutes before he had started talking to Lena. But there was now no sign of either of them.

Following the discovery of Lena's remains the following morning, two police officers were dispatched to Chikatilo's family apartment but were immediately assured by his wife that he'd been with her and their children throughout the previous evening after returning from work via the station where the little girl had gone missing. Chikatilo's wife later claimed she had felt compelled to provide a false alibi for her husband to preserve her marriage to him and because she was also extremely scared of him. Given this alibi, the officers concluded that there was no way Chikatilo was involved in the disappearance of Lena.

With an entire community in shock about the brutal murder of an innocent child, Rostov police decided to go down the most predictable investigative route of all in their bid to find the killer. With no forensic evidence at the scene of the murder, they began trawling through the files of all known sex offenders in the region, as well as studying the registries of the region's mentally ill people.

Eventually, investigators pinpointed a 25-year-old sex offender called Aleksandr Kravchenko, who had one previous rape conviction. He was hauled in by detectives and quickly confessed to the first killing committed by Chikatilo. It was only later that the interrogation methods used by the police were revealed to have been heavy-handed, to say the least. At that time, Soviet law enforcement was notorious for regularly forcing false confessions out of prisoners through torture and intimidation.

Some detectives inside the Rostov police told colleagues they were far from convinced of the alleged guilt of suspect Kravchenko. But the officers who had interviewed Kravchenko insisted he was their man. The normally secretive authorities proudly publicized his arrest, as they were convinced it would help bring some calm back to the city and deter any more similar types of killings.

Chikatilo later recalled being bemused when he read about Kravchenko's alleged involvement in the newspapers. But he insisted that, despite the other man's arrest, he had resisted the urge to go out and find a new victim, after feeling guilt-ridden and confused by his first murder. He claimed that for more than two years he resisted the urge to re-live that first killing. Then he picked up a newspaper to find that Kravchenko had been executed. He interpreted this as a green light to kill again. He explained: "It was as if there was some higher power helping me and urging me to go out and find more victims. In my mind there was no other explanation for the police charging that innocent man and executing him."

On 3 September 1981, Chikatilo began a conversation with 17-year-old Larisa Tkachenko at a train station in the suburbs of Rostov. He persuaded her to accompany him to a nearby wood, where he stuffed her mouth with dirt and leaves to prevent her from crying out before strangling and stabbing her.

Over the following 18 months, Chikatilo befriended more young people at train stations and bus stops before luring some of them into nearby forest areas, where he'd attack them, attempt rape and use his knife to mutilate them. In a number of cases, he ate his victims' sexual organs, as well as removing other body parts, such as the tips of their noses or tongues. But his most chilling "calling card" was removing his victims' eyeballs. It was an act which Chikatilo later attributed to a belief that those he attacked retained an imprint of his face in their eyes, even after death.

The killer continually read about the murders in the city newspapers with detached bemusement, since none of them were being connected to each other by the police. Often, he watched TV news reports while sitting at home with his wife and two children and chuckled to himself when another mystery killing was revealed. After the first three or four murders weren't solved or linked to each other, Chikatilo became convinced that no one was going to stop him.

During 1982, journalists in the city wrote articles claiming that the police did not try very hard to connect the murders as they didn't want to admit that they'd sent the wrong man to the firing squad after the first killing. One reporter explained: "It was much easier for them to blame that sex offender for that one murder and not connect it to the rest."

Chikatilo – like many serial killers – developed his own system and skill set as his killing rampage continued. Besides posing as a teacher, he sometimes told his victims he was a travelling businessman, with that official-looking briefcase. It actually contained a secret "murder kit", which included an 8-inch knife, a jar of Vaseline, some rope and a dirty towel. He'd worked out a legitimate excuse for carrying the items if he was ever stopped by police. He'd say he was out hunting jackrabbits. The Vaseline was needed to wipe down his blade and the rope was essential to hang the dead rabbits on a stick to keep them fresh for eating.

As the body count mounted, wild rumours spread around Rostov about the murders being part of a foreign-inspired plot to destabilize the region. Others projected the killer as being some kind of werewolf. Local communist party officials tried to play down the stories. They wanted information to only come from official news outlets so they could control what was being said and thus play down the atrocities occurring right across the region, which put the motherland in a bad light. Mere suggestions of serial killings, or even child abuse, were suppressed by the state-controlled media in the interests of public order. There had been no mention of the eye mutilation of all the victims, either, as this arguably linked the cases.

In truth, the Rostov police were completely baffled by the killings that started with Chitakilo's first victim in late 1978 and continued right the way through 1983. It felt to them like an impossible task, and some investigators quickly ran out of steam. They had little or no previous experience of these sorts of crimes and had no idea how to conduct such murder enquiries.

As a result, a detective from Moscow called Major Mikhail Fetisov was drafted in to assume control of the investigation in the middle of 1983. Recognizing that a serial killer was undoubtedly on the loose, Fetisov assigned a specialist forensic officer called Viktor Burakov to head the on-the-ground investigation into the killings. He quickly established that the killer had blood type AB thanks to semen samples collected from two murder scenes. A few strands of identical grey hair were also retrieved. Forensic expert Burakov insisted they should compare the semen samples with any potential suspects, and the entire investigation was finally ramped up. But those semen samples taken from two of the murder scenes could not be directly compared with Chitakilo's samples, because he'd never been arrested in the past.

Meanwhile, the re-booted police investigation led to the apprehension of other murderers and more than two hundred rapists, after police tracked down every known offender and suspect on their books. But in many ways, this was a distraction, as it resulted in officers being swamped with unsolved crime investigations unconnected to the case.

In early 1984, police chiefs became side-tracked once again when informants insisted that criminal gangs of mentally ill youths in Rostov had been responsible for all of the murders committed by Chikatilo. Members of two of these gangs were eventually rounded up and jailed for various offences, but nothing could be proved in relation to the actual murders.

Chikatilo remained at liberty and his appetite for killing was as strong as ever, so the killings continued. During the first eight months of 1984, he killed fifteen further victims, and this disturbing surge in killings forced Rostov police and their colleagues already drafted in from Moscow to further step up their efforts to catch him. They announced plans to blood-test nearly 200,000 male motorists. Officers also placed hidden cameras in many of the city's railway stations, disguised policewomen as drifters and used dozens of officers dressed up as railroad workers and mushroom pickers to monitor the most likely places where the killer might strike next.

One ambitious young detective called Lt. Col. Alexander Zanasovsky pressed his superiors, including lead investigator Major Mikhail Fetisov, to allow him to go to some of the transport hubs where they believed the killer had picked up victims. Zanasovsky worked on the simple premise that: "The killer would always go back to where he has had success before." In the later summer of 1984, Zanasovsky spent some days watching people at bus and railway stations with no success. Occasionally a man would appear to be a suspect due to his behaviour, but after being brought in for an interview with Zanasovsky, they would soon be cleared after providing evidence of their movements.

Then, on 13 September 1984, Zanasovsky and another undercover colleague noticed a respectable-looking older man approaching women at a bus station in a Rostov suburb. He was also seen rubbing himself up against two females queuing for tickets. When Zanasovsky confronted the middle-aged man, he said that he was bored, and that, as a former teacher, he chatted with young people by habit. It was a bit strange, but with nothing more to go on, Zanasovsky let the man go.

A few weeks later, Zanasovsky saw the man doing exactly the same thing once again in another bus station. Zanasovsky recalled: "This time I thought, 'You won't get away from me.'"

When Zanasovsky arrested the middle-aged man, he noticed drops of sweat the size of raindrops on his forehead. "I had never seen that before," he said. "That was not the reaction of an innocent man."

Following the suspect's arrest, police found rope, wire and a long knife in his briefcase. But back at the police station, they failed to match a blood type sample from the man to the blood type in the semen recovered earlier by forensics at the scene of two of the killings. Without enough evidence to charge him with murder, Andrei Chikatilo was released. Zanasovsky – haunted by what happened that night – recalled: "I thought he was our man. In fact, I was certain, but we didn't have enough to hold him and his name was removed from the long list of suspects tied to the murders."

While Chikatilo was in custody, police had also discovered that he was wanted for stealing from a former employer. As a result – in December 1984 – he was actually sentenced to three months in prison. It was a small price to pay for Chikatilo. All his earlier fears about being brought to justice evaporated when police told him his blood and fluid sample tests had cleared him of any involvement in the killings. He eventually tried to imply that certain corrupt police officers had knowingly let him off and encouraged him to "cull" Rostov's homeless drifters because they were giving the city a bad name. Inside his deluded mind, Chikatilo believed police had given him a "licence" to kill these people, but nothing could be further from the truth.

While Chikatilo was in prison during the autumn and early winter of 1984, Lt. Col. Alexander Zanasovsky continued to diligently research his suspect's background and habits, despite colleagues refusing to help him after pointing out that Chikatilo had been cleared by the forensic evidence. Zanasovsky eventually dug up paperwork referring to Chikatilo's tarnished reputation as a teacher and how he'd lost jobs for molesting children. Additionally, he discovered that Chikatilo's most recent job had involved travelling around the country obtaining supplies for a local factory, which meant he was constantly on business trips away from home. That meant he had ample opportunities while on his own to launch attacks. He also lived near some of the forests where victims had been killed, after they'd been charmed by him at the travel hubs he used to travel to and from work.

Following Chikatilo's release from his three-month prison sentence in March 1985, he got a new job as a travelling buyer for a train company, based in Novocherkassk. No one knows how quickly he started attacking new victims, but within months – in August 1985 – he is known to have murdered two young women in separate incidents. Both were very similar to his earlier slayings.

After that, the attacks appeared to stop for more than two years. Many detectives were convinced the killer had either gone to prison for other offences or, better still, died. On the other hand, his victims at that time may simply have "disappeared" and were never actually linked to Chikatilo.

But early in 1988, Chikatilo began targeting victims on the streets, rather than inside transport stations. He had correctly presumed police surveillance teams would be covering those locations. Over the following two years, Chikatilo murdered at least nineteen more people, most of them picked up by him in public places such as streets and in alleyways.

Despite the obvious danger, he still preferred transport hubs, because that was where potential targets usually had no friends or family to greet them and little money. That made them much easier to lure away to the forest. It was a reckless move, but by this time Chikatilo didn't really care. He later claimed that he had remained convinced the police would never catch him.

Meanwhile many citizens in Rostov had other things on their mind. The entire Soviet Union was under threat as an institution. New communist party leader Mikael Gorbachev's controversial Glasnot modernizing measures were putting more public pressure on law enforcement to catch killers such as Chikatilo, to prove that the existing communist system did work efficiently. So police patrols were stepped up in Rostov. More undercover officers were dispatched onto the streets and into transport stations across the region.

In August 1989, forensic detective Viktor Burakov – brought in earlier by Moscow detective Major Mikhail Fetisov – approached the city's best-known criminal psychiatrist, Alexander Bukhanovsky. After years of Chikatilo being mostly ignored by detectives, Bukhanovsky immediately came up with an in-depth profile of the killer, concluding that he was a "necro-sadist" – someone who achieved sexual gratification from the suffering and death of others. The psychiatrist's profile also stated that the suspect was an educated man. Chikatilo had a university degree.

The expert said he was middle-aged, tall and strong, neatly dressed, wore glasses, carried a briefcase containing a knife, was a known sexual pervert, and suffered from impotence, with a history of sexual molestation and personal sexual problems. Dr Bukhanovsky's estimate that the killer was aged between 45 and 50 was significantly older than what police had continually claimed. Detectives also informed Dr Bukhanovsky that the killer had removed his victims' eyes. He concluded that this had most likely been done as the killer feared that his own image would be caught like a passport photo in the liquid darkness of their pupils.

Dr Bukhanovsky was soon working alongside the team hunting the Rostov killer. He considered the investigation to be very personal as this psychopath was murdering in the city he and his family called home. Bukhanovsky recalled: "I feared for my own little girl's life. And I lived just two miles from some of the locations where he had been killing."

On 6 November 1990, Chikatilo was spotted by a police patrol leaving the woodland on the edge of Rostov. Officers stopped him and asked for his personal details. They let him go after he showed them his genuine identity card, which convinced them he had nothing to hide. He'd actually just killed a teenager called Sveta Korostik.

Less than two weeks later – on 19 November 1990 – another police patrol specifically assigned to cover the area close to a different train station saw Chikatilo emerge from nearby woods and stop to clean his boots and coat in a puddle. As an officer approached Chikatilo, he noticed a smear of blood on his cheek and what appeared to be a deep cut on his finger. When the patrolman quizzed Chikatilo, he smiled and explained he'd fallen over after hearing a bear. When the officer asked to look at his identity card, he happily obliged. The officer surmised that if he had been up to no good, he would not have been so co-operative. He did not detain Chikatilo.

The following day, the body of a young girl was discovered in those same woods. Chikatilo's name only came up after the local chief of police demanded that his officers provide all the details of any suspicious individuals seen in the vicinity of the killing during the previous 24 hours. Officers then discovered that Chikatilo had also been stopped some days previously. Further digging into the police records revealed that he'd been questioned back in 1984. At the same time, a member of the public contacted the police to say they'd seen a man matching Chikatilo's description trying to force a boy off a train with him on the same evening that he'd killed his most recent victim.

An immediate re-examination of Chikatilo's blood sample was ordered by forensic detective Viktor Burakov. His blood type, type A, was different to the type connected to the semen recovered from earlier murder scenes (type AB). It was only then discovered that he was actually a member of a minority group known as "non-secretors", whose blood type can not be established by anything other than a direct blood sample.

Today, more sophisticated forensic techniques would have completely overridden this defect in the system because they would have been able to properly break down a semen sample. But this wasn't the case in the late 1980s. One senior investigator who worked on the case at that time recalled: "The law enforcement bodies were at fault mainly in that they relied too much on the biological facts. What did we learn? That you have to check everyone." A number of renowned American forensic experts have since alleged that Russian police technicians had handled the samples so sloppily in the first place that it was no surprise that Chikatilo could not be linked to the murders.

That same day – 20 November 1990 – Chikatilo was arrested at his family home in Rostov. He refused to let officers into his apartment but readily offered his wrists to be handcuffed, providing the detectives promised not to disturb his family. After he'd arrived at police headquarters, the suspected serial killer was locked in a basement cell after he refused to respond to any of the specific allegations. He had no idea that detectives had finally matched his DNA to the samples earlier found at those two murder scenes.

When Chikatilo's wife Fayina was informed by two police officers that her husband had been taken away for questioning, she initially thought he'd been detained after taking part in public protests about some new garages being constructed in the neighbourhood where they lived with their children.

Back at the city's main police station, their suspect repeatedly refused to talk to detectives. He did, however, agree to be interviewed by a psychiatrist after officers convinced him they needed to analyze his mind from a scientific perspective in order to decide if he would face criminal charges.

Chikatilo seemed almost flattered by the attention of such an expert, as he saw it as an opportunity to try and ensure he was diagnosed as insane, which would help him avoid a lifelong prison sentence or possibly the death penalty.

At the start of his interview with the psychiatrist, Chikatilo tried to explain away his crimes by dressing them up in bigger issues, as investigators watched him through a two-way mirror. As one detective recalled: "He was such a narcissist that he actually thought the psychiatrist would be impressed by his analysis of himself and how his victims were just poor, irrelevant people on life's scrapheap who deserved to die. He really believed that this twisted logic would help him avoid a death sentence." The suspect calmly informed the psychiatrist: "Seeing them on the streets, I began to wonder whether these low-class elements had the right to exist." He made it sound to the psychiatrist like he was helping his victims, whom he continually described as "young and bored and naïve".

Chikatilo's claim that he only ever targeted homeless drifters was nothing more than a thinly veiled excuse for murdering anyone he could lay his hands on. His victims had actually included students from secure families, as well as kind and trusting young men and women and innocent young children left unattended for just a few moments in train and bus stations, like his first victim, nine-year-old Lena Zakotnova.

As Chikatilo opened up to the police psychiatrist, he was actually gradually confessing to all his crimes, although he didn't seem to appreciate what he was doing. He told the psychiatrist he considered himself a charming character. It was clear to the psychiatrist and watching detectives that he believed he had such a magnetic personality that it had enabled him to persuade his victims to happily follow him into dark forests on their own and that it would now help him convince the authorities he was insane. Chikatilo boasted: "I'd just say to all of them, 'Let's go, let's have something to eat' or whatever. They were everywhere, at every step. I didn't have to search hard for them."

Other criminologists concluded that Chikatilo's reaction was probably also sparked by his own uncontrollable jealousy when it came to the freedom enjoyed by many of his victims. It reminded him of how impotent he was and also forced him to think about how badly damaged he was after his own troubled childhood. Then, completely out of the blue, he surprised the psychiatrist who interviewed him that first day in custody by announcing: "I didn't see why they should enjoy sex when I couldn't manage it. They had no right to it like I did."

The psychiatrist was careful not to ridicule Chikatilo's attitude by nodding each time he spoke as if he agreed with the criminal's chilling excuses for mass murder. "That's when I was certain he'd confess to everything," one detective – who watched that first interview through the two-way mirror – later explained. "He actually thought the psychiatrist was on his side and that he'd managed to manipulate him into agreeing that his victims deserved to die. He believed that would convince the psychiatrist he was insane and not responsible for the crimes he'd committed." The same detective also recalled: "I felt sick that he thought he could manipulate us and that psychiatrist but we all had a job to do and we had to put such thoughts to one side. The only thing that mattered was that we owed it to those victims to make sure Chikalito was properly brought to justice for his crimes."

In the middle of this extraordinary interview, Chikatilo began turning and smiling at the two-way mirror, behind which were half a dozen detectives gathered in a group watching and listening. Chikalito then provided intimate details of 36 of the murders he'd committed. Afterwards, he sat back in his chair and turned to smile at the two-way mirror.

"There were more than that, you know," Chikalito said quietly, still looking into the mirror. He then sighed heavily and went into detail about 17 more killings that the police did not even know about. After he'd finished describing the latest killings, he looked once more into the two-way mirror and said softly: "I was like a crazed wolf. I just turned into a beast, into a wild animal." Then, titling his head, he smiled. "What I did was not for sexual pleasure. Rather it brought me some peace of mind."

Chikatilo admitted to almost 60 murders that day, although only 53 of them could be independently verified. It was almost double the number of cases the police had originally intended charging him with. Yet he still believed he had the police eating out of his hand. Another of the police detectives who'd watched him through the two-way mirror recalled: "He had this smug look on his face almost as if he'd got one over on all of us by telling us about a load of murders we knew nothing about. For a few moments it felt that he was right but the reality eventually dawned on him that his boasting meant we could now help those victims and their families to at least rest in peace."

In the police station, a new team of investigators took over talking to Chikatilo after the psychiatrist announced he was emotionally and physically exhausted after hours of listening to his chilling confessions. This time, the suspect did not object to the police interviewing him. The key to wrapping up the investigation was to continue encouraging Chikatilo to confess after he'd fully accepted the detectives taking over in the interview room. He'd deduced that he was providing evidence that would label him as insane and that would enable him to avoid a death sentence.

One detective who was part of the team that interviewed Chikatilo recalled: "At certain moments it felt as if he was writing the script of his life. He gave us highs, lows, lots of colourful detail and each time he said something particularly gruesome, he'd stop for a moment and watch our faces for a reaction before carrying on."

As the interview continued, he provided increasingly graphic descriptions of the violent acts he'd committed. On those occasions, he seemed to shake with excitement as he flashed back to incidents. He admitted to detectives: "The thrill from the anticipation of what I was about to do was immense. In some ways it was like a fever. Then once I got them in the woods I knew I could do anything I wanted to them."

Chikatilo also agreed to take the police to the sites where many of those extra killings had occurred to help provide irrefutable evidence of his crimes.

When it came to discussing his wife Fayina, he became extremely agitated and protective, though. He insisted to investigators that he always told her that the factory where he worked had been forcing him to load filthy crates and that was why he often had wounds and marks on his body when he came home at night.

* * *

However, Chikatilo's bid to appear mentally unfit was declared a sham by the psychiatrist who questioned him during that first marathon interviewing session following his arrest, and he was told he would stand trial. Chikatilo looked crestfallen when informed of the news by his court-appointed lawyer.

His trail began on 14 April 1992 at courtroom number five of the Rostov Provincial Court. There were genuine fears that the accused's mood would soon darken as the realization that he could end up in front of a firing squad began to dawn on him. For that reason, he was held in a metal cage specifically designed to keep him apart from everyone in the court, especially the relatives of his many victims. TV news footage of Chikatilo pacing up and down inside the cage with his head shaven made him look terrifying. Sometimes he stopped to turn and stare at certain individuals, which they said sent a shiver up their spines.

With the Soviet Union's brand of communism having recently crumbled, the rest of the world began asking whether Chikatilo really was a serial killer or just a bespectacled schoolteacher who'd been framed by inefficient communist law enforcement agents under pressure to prosecute someone for the mass killings. There were genuine fears outside Russia that he was nothing more than a fall guy arrested and charged by the Soviets just to show how good they were at detective work.

Throughout the trial, the local, mostly state-controlled media took a different stance. Incensed by his crimes, they referred to Chikatilo as "The Maniac". And as the court case continued, his behaviour ranged from bored to outrageous. Sometimes he'd sing and talk gibberish. On one occasion, he dropped his trousers and defiantly waved his genitals at the assembled crowd in the court's public gallery.

During the trial itself, Judge Leonid Akubzhanov proved less than impartial by regularly overruling defence lawyers on specific points of law. Many present that day presumed that Chikatilo's guilt had been a foregone conclusion ever since the day he was first arrested. Judge Akubzhanov was also permitted to interrogate the defendant himself during the early stages of the trial. He asked Chikatilo over and over again for simple explanations for the horrific acts he'd committed in an effort to try and discover what drove him to kill. The judge insisted he wanted the court to understand how a person could be so utterly without conscience.

"Didn't you imagine what excruciating pain it would cause your victims when you bit off their tongues?" Judge Akubzhanov asked Chikatilo. "I've seen hundreds of corpses, but I've never seen any like this. We want to understand your psychology. Were you thinking, 'I can make anyone I want a victim,' or what? For one minute of pleasure, you demanded the life of a child. Didn't you think about that?" Chikatilo refused to deal with such issues and mumbled simply: "I can't explain." One detective recalled: "That response was typical of the man. He couldn't look inside himself and appreciate the lives and families he'd destroyed. It wasn't on his agenda to ever care. Chikatilo lived in a world dominated by himself and no one else." The psychologist who'd initially examined Chikatilo following his arrest told the court: "He understands that what he did was bad, that he killed people. But that doesn't mean he's sorry. The judge appealed to his conscience, but he was only sorry for himself."

Chikatilo was eventually permitted to give a rambling monologue in court that lasted nearly two hours. He portrayed himself as a long-suffering, persecuted man driven over the edge by his horrible childhood. There was also the humiliation of his own sexual impotence, which he claimed resulted in problems at work and at home. He also blamed some of his killings on his endless business trips, which he said enabled him to avoid his domestic life and led to him being driven by his disturbing sexual urges.

He attempted to elicit sympathy from the court by claiming that he was constantly haunted by his own failures. He said: "I dreamed of a big political career and ended up with this nothing life, except what I found in stations and on trains." He told the court in a detached voice that when he went into the forest with his knife it became his only actual success. The court was stunned into silence when Chikatilo added: "When I used my knife, it brought psychological relief." He even openly referred to his own "perverted sexuality".

Not surprisingly, many of the victims' bereaved family members who attended the trial sought revenge for what had happened to their loved ones. Paulina Ishutina – whose 20-year-old daughter had been brutally killed by Chikatilo – told journalists outside the court: "Why bother trying him? If they gave him to me, I'd tear him apart. I'd gouge out his eyes and cut him up. I'd do everything to him that he did to my daughter." She added: "My daughter had 46 knife wounds, her womb was cut out. Why did he do that? What did he need with it? How can you torment someone like that? I can't understand it. It all just won't fit into my head. Every day we talk through it all, and it still doesn't make sense."

Towards the end of his trial, Chikatilo underwent new psychiatric tests and was officially re-classified as a schizoid psychopath due to what experts described as his rich inner life. But he was still sane enough to be tried for the murders, they said. One analyst explained: "While he imagined himself in lofty roles, such as that of a partisan – rebel fighter – in real life he called himself an idiot, a good-for-nothing. But all this self-criticism was a ploy to help him avoid responsibility for his crimes." One detective recalled: "Chikatilo was constantly trying over and over again to manipulate the psychiatrists by being self-effacing but he didn't mean one word of it. It was just an act to try and convince the court he was insane."

Chikatilo's trial lasted until the end of August 1992, when the judge announced to the court that the verdict would be revealed in two months, in accordance with the new legal system that had just evolved from the ashes of communism.

On 15 October 1992, Chikatilo was found guilty of 52 of the 53 murder charges he faced. He was sentenced to death for each of those murders. The court heard that he had tortured, slaughtered and mutilated 21 boys, 14 girls and 18 young women in what was described by prosecutors as "an odyssey of murder and unspeakable sadism".

Immediately after his sentencing, Chikatilo launched an appeal claiming that the most recent psychiatric tests – which had labelled him a schizoid psychopath – shouldn't have led to him continuing to stand trial. It seemed a realistic defence strategy, so there was a genuine fear that the conviction might be reversed.

Then there was Chikatilo's wife, Fayina. Many detectives remain convinced to this day that she must have known what her husband was doing. One officer confronted her on behalf of the victims' families outside the courthouse after the end of the trial: "It can't be you didn't know. He would come home dirty as an animal, bloody. You must have known." Fayina always categorically denied having had even a hint of a suspicion that her husband was a mass killer. She said she'd given him an alibi following his first kill after being convinced he could not be a murderer. But by doing that she had – albeit unintentionally – helped enable Chikatilo to go on and murder at least 60 more victims.

Fayina never publicly revealed her own feelings upon hearing during the trial that her husband got more sexual gratification from stabbing his victims than he ever had in bed with her. There is a suggestion that she struggled to accept that the man who'd been so gentle to her was capable of such heinous acts. She told one reporter following the trial: "I could never imagine him being able to hurt one person, let alone 53. He could never hurt anyone."

Chikatilo's long-standing loyalty to his wife took a strange twist following his conviction, though, when he alleged to one detective that he was afraid of Fayina, claiming that he would cower in a corner whenever she yelled at him at home. Investigators believed that this was just yet more manipulation from Chikatilo, as he made a last, desperate bid to avoid execution.

Fayina and the couple's two children eventually changed their names and moved away from Rostov following a number of death threats, which many believe came from the families of his victims.

* * *

Chikalito's appeal against his death sentence failed after experts insisted he'd tried to manipulate the court, despite being labelled a schizoid psychopath, and therefore was still fully responsible for his actions.

On Valentine's Day 1994, he was prepared by prison guards to be executed. It had been 16 months since he'd been found guilty.

Minutes before he was due to die, Chikalito asked that his eyes be removed from his corpse. He claimed he wanted them to be donated for medical research but admitted to two prison officers that he believed his eyes might "record" his execution. It was the same excuse he always claimed for removing the eyes of his victims. One detective explained: "That was his last attempt at overturning his execution. He thought the eyes issue would convince the authorities he was insane after all. They didn't fall for his trickery thank God."

Later that same day, Chikalito's life was ended with a shot in the back of his head.

In 2009, his only son Yuri was charged with rape in addition to several lesser charges. A few months after that, he was also arrested for attempted murder. After that, Russian authorities threw a veil of secrecy around the case, so no other details have ever been disclosed about it.

CHAPTER FOUR

THE HUNTER

**Uzynagash to Maibulak Highway, Uzynagash,
Kazakhstan, 24 January 1979**

Nikolai Dzhumagaliev had a habit of breathing very noisily
when he was out hunting. Most put it down to the anticipation
and energy he exerted while stalking his prey in the forests and
mountains overlooking his isolated home in this sparsely populated area of Kazakhstan. It was also due to the oversized glossy
tin plate of dentures he'd had to wear ever since he was a teenager. These were extremely disarming to anyone the 27-year-
old met because they glittered, especially at night when they'd
reflect off any bright lights. There was also Dzhumagaliev's facial
hair. He had tufts of it growing out of various parts of his face,
and those who encountered him at the time said it gave him the
appearance of being a neanderthal man from prehistoric times.

His father once told him that his metal teeth were the
main reason why Dzhumagaliev sometimes struggled to catch

any animals while out hunting. "The animals see the glitter of your teeth and they run," Dzhumagaliev's father told his son dryly. "You'd be better off without them." Dzhumagaliev disagreed with his father, although he never said this to his face in case he got a clout for his troubles. He'd had a lot of problems making friends after he'd lost his original teeth during what he later claimed was a school playground fight. He believed that, without his metal fangs, he'd never find a good woman to marry and have children with.

He thought a lot about such things while out night-hunting, and that stirred him into fantasizing about all sorts of sordid activities, often revolving around sexual relations with women. Sometimes he'd spot women walking along the isolated tracks on the edge of the forest close to his cabin and wonder if any of them might be prepared to date him if he stopped and asked them. But Dzhumagaliev could never actually work up the courage to approach them.

On the bitterly cold evening of 25 January 1979 – with temperatures having plunged to minus 10 – loner Dzhumagaliev was out hunting close to the deserted Uzynagash to Maibulak road, which was more of a dirt track than a highway. Snapping his eyes 360 degrees in all directions, Dzhumagaliev spotted something about 300 metres ahead of him on the track. She was a 17-year-old Seventh Day Adventist, and she was alone.

Dzhumagaliev later said that he felt his heart pounding with excitement the moment he noticed her and that that prompted him to begin running at high speed towards her. The young woman only heard his footsteps thumping on the gritty track when he was just a few yards behind her. As she turned around, she noticed his dark eyes and those shining metal teeth and started to run for her life. Dzhumagaliev soon caught up with her and threw her to the ground. He put his arm around her neck. But when she desperately tried to claw at his hand, he squeezed tighter. Dzhumagaliev's breathing got louder and more uneven as he stood behind her choking the air out of her while pressing himself hard against her body.

He grasped her neck until she crumpled to the ground, apparently unconscious. Dzhumagaliev recalled: "I had a plan and I needed to get on with it." As he dragged her by the back of her neck across the track, the heels of her shoes scraped the gravel and she recovered consciousness and cried for help. He punched her in the stomach so hard that she doubled up in pain on the ground. This enabled him to pull her across the mossy bank next to the track, his boots crunching in the brittle snow.

Dzhumagaliev dragged her to a landfill site less than 50 feet away. He'd been there many times before while out hunting. The young woman had stopped resisting. Instead, she smiled up at him, and this disarmed him completely. She started pulling her long dress up to expose her legs in the hope it might stop him doing something even worse.

Dzhumagaliev later said he was disgusted by her actions as he wanted to be the one who decided when he would do anything to her. Her offer of sex made him feel dizzy with anger. He flashed open his thick winter anorak so she could see the big hunting knife in a holster attached to his trouser belt.

He was about to take it out when he heard the distant, rattling sound of a motor vehicle on the road ahead. The blur of its headlights coming towards them in the darkness told him it was the village bus, and there was a bus stop just 20 yards from where he was standing.

Dzhumagaliev threw himself and the teenage girl to the ground and pulled her close to him. She was by this time frozen with fear. He put his hand over her mouth and pressed hard against her body, which helped make him warmer. Their eyes were just inches apart. He stared deep into her as the bus approached. She was too terrified to do anything because she knew he'd take that knife out and use it without hesitation.

The bus didn't stop and continued its journey. There was just one passenger – an old lady – sitting right at the back as Dzhumagaliev watched from his vantage point. Once the bus was completely out of sight, Dzhumagaliev knelt over the woman and roughly pulled off all her clothes, including her underwear. She didn't try to stop him.

He lay her out flat on the frozen ground and stood up before tilting his head while examining her naked body. Then he climbed on top of her and raped her. When he'd finished, he got off her and removed his hunting knife from its holster and held it in one hand. She was sobbing. He looked down at her and spat in her anguished face. As she tried to wipe the spittle from her cheek, he knelt down on the ground and pressed the point of the blade into the side of her neck just under her ear and motioned for her to be quiet by putting his finger to his lips.

She tried not to breathe, let alone move, aware that if she did then the tip of that knife would puncture her skin. Dzhumagaliev stared into her pale, watery eyes, which were open wide and staring up at the clear night sky. The moonlight bounced off his dentures as he continued looking down at her. She was paralyzed with fear.

His eyes narrowed and he pushed the point of the blade in about half an inch and left it there for a few seconds as droplets of blood started seeping out. Slowly, he ripped the knife handle across her neck. By the time he'd reached the exact same point underneath her other ear, she was already dead.

He threw the knife on the ground next to his backpack and stood over her for a few seconds admiring his grotesque handiwork while breathing noisily. Then he got down on both knees and leaned in close to where the gaping wound around her neck was gushing blood and began lapping noisily at it with his tongue. The warm blood tasted so good to him that it aroused him once again, so he straddled her naked, punctured body again and penetrated her.

Dzhumagaliev later recalled that it wasn't as satisfying as when she'd been alive, so he pulled out of her and pushed his penis into the gaping stab wound in her neck as her head leaned at a grotesque angle.

Afterwards, he picked up his knife from where he'd thrown it on the ground and began slicing strips of flesh off her breasts. He had smears of blood on his cheeks and there was a large droplet in the corner of his lip. More blood stained his shiny white enamel fangs. He wasn't finished yet.

He plunged the knife into her lower abdomen and forced it up into her before slicing a hole out of her flesh. Then he shoved his hand inside her and removed her ovaries before separating the pelvis and hips. He knew from hunting and eating animals that these were the best bits. Having laid all the "meat" out on the frozen ground, he neatly folded each piece and placed them in his backpack.

Minutes afterwards, he was strolling along that same narrow track whistling happily to himself. His first prey had been relatively easy to kill and she was, he hoped, just the right weight to provide him with what he required.

Back home 10 minutes later, Dzhumagaliev walked into his kitchen, took out a frying pan and threw a lump of white lard into it before firing up the gas ring. He then went to the kitchen table and took out from his backpack a couple of strips of flesh from her breast area and dropped them into the bubbling pan. Within 30 seconds, he turned them over with a spatula. Half a minute after that, he placed them on a plate and carefully cut the meat up into small pieces with a sharp, serrated kitchen knife. Then he ate them.

Dzhumagaliev recalled that he didn't find the first few pieces of human meat particularly appetizing, but he didn't want to waste them after being taught as a child never to leave anything on his plate. "After a few more mouthfuls I got used to the taste and rather liked it," he recalled.

After his meal, Dzhumagaliev took some other body parts out of the backpack and pickled them in three huge glass jars that contained vinegar. Other pieces of the woman's body were put through a noisy meat grinder and rolled into *pelemi* (Russian dumplings) with flour. He placed them on a plate and put them in the fridge.

He then fired up the grill and carefully placed the heart and kidneys on the griddle under the flames. He stopped to inspect them after a few minutes by prodding at the pieces with a fork. Deciding they were not yet sufficiently cooked, he turned up the grill and gave them another five minutes. Dzhumagaliev later said they were much tastier than the earlier pieces of human meat he'd eaten.

The remains of that young woman lasted Dzhumagaliev a month. He later explained that his only complaint was that the meat contained too much fat for his liking, so he'd had to drain a lot of it off before sitting down to eat. He ended up using a lot of that human fat for cooking when he feasted on the rest of her remains over the following weeks. Dzhumagaliev said it greatly improved the taste and texture of the meat.

* * *

Kazakhstan is the ninth largest land-locked territory in the world. There are vast swathes of deserted lowlands stretching for many hundreds of miles between cities and mountains. Shortages of food have haunted this region on and off for centuries.

Citizens had long since grown used to recognizing the classic signs of starvation in both boys and girls. This included big tufts of facial hair, similar in appearance to what had sprouted from Dzhumagaliev's face from an early age. Other symptoms of starvation included male impotency and irregular menstrual cycles in women. During various famines and the Second World War, the Soviet government had only been able to provide its citizens with meagre supplies of food. In Kazakhstan, this had resulted in many families resorting to desperate measures to find food.

At least 5,000 people from Kazakhstan were arrested for cannibalism during the 1940s and 1950s. Some parents had no choice but to feed their children the human flesh of dead relatives. Even today many Kazakhstan natives distinguish between two different types of cannibalism: the first is eating the flesh of a corpse when someone is already dead, the second is specifically killing another human being in order to eat them.

So these hardships were commonplace by the time Nikolai Dzhumagaliev was born in 1952, in Uzynagash, 50 kilometres from the bustling, densely populated city of Almaty, capital of the Kazakh Soviet Socialist Republic, as the region was then known.

The third of four children, Dzhumagaliev and his family were very poor. His father was a Kazakh and his mother from Belarus. Dzhumagaliev's childhood hero was legendary local warlord Ghengis Khan. Dzhumagaliev proudly told anyone who would listen that he was a descendant of Genghis Khan. Or, at least, that's what he claimed to be.

The brutal twelfth-century warlord was a long-standing hero to many people in the area of Kazakhstan where Dzhumagaliev was brought up. He'd conquered much of the region and built one of the biggest empires the world has ever seen. Ghengis Khan had a much more bloody and brutal reputation elsewhere in Russia and Asia. If anyone disobeyed Khan, he'd have them crushed to death under huge boulders, or molten lead poured into their eyes and ears. Yet many centuries after his reign of terror, many of Kazakhstan's citizens still lived in awe of him. One of Dzhumagaliev's school classmates recalled: "Dzhumagaliev used to get really nasty if you laughed at his obsession with Ghengis Khan. He worshipped Khan's role in our history and proudly modelled himself on him."

Dzhumagaliev attended what was known in the Soviet Union as a railway school. All of its pupils were the children of railway workers like his father. Dzhumagaliev was eventually called up for mandatory military service in the chemical defence corps at two Soviet armed forces bases in Samarkand and Otar. This put him on the front line of the Soviets' controversial chemical defence system. Dzhumagaliev regularly handled deadly substances including nerve gas, and some have since claimed that these chemicals affected his personality as he became a much colder character and more of a loner during his national service.

Dzhumagaliev was also very determined to further himself in life. He told his few army friends that he planned to be the first member of his family to study at university once he returned to civilian life. On leaving the armed forces in 1973, he applied to enter Kazakh university and also lined up a chauffeuring job to pay for his college expenses. Dzhumagaliev failed to get either position.

Bitterly disappointed by these setbacks, Dzhumagaliev – now aged 20 – set off on his travels across the Urals, Siberia and Murmansk. He intended paying for this travelling and accomodation by working various blue-collar jobs along the way. This work ended up including a brief period in the Soviet Union's poorly paid merchant navy. He was prone to sea sickness, so left the service after just a few months. Dzhumagaliev ended up also driving a bulldozer and overseeing the dispatch of goods from a huge warehouse.

In many ways, he'd become a classic nomad, travelling from region to region across the Soviet Union, in a similar fashion to his great hero Genghis Khan. Dzhumagaliev cleaned up his appearance following comments about his facial hair and those metal false teeth. He later said he'd wanted to make himself more employable and attractive to women.

In 1977, after a few years travelling, Dzhumagaliev returned to his home town of Uzynagash and got a job as a firefighter. It should have been a step up for him as it gave him some standing in the local community. He also saw it as a way to impress women and improve his virtually non-existent love life. But within months, he was diagnosed with two sexually transmitted diseases, syphilis and trichomoniasis.

Dzhumagaliev immediately blamed women as a whole for his embarrassing health problems and began developing an intense hatred of them. His moodiness – already edgy due to the chemicals he'd handled while in the army – worsened considerably. Dzhumagaliev never openly admitted how he got those STDs, but associates at that time recalled that his only sexual partners were prostitutes and a couple of supposedly "easy" women from the centre of town. Family and friends noticed that Dzhumagaliev became increasingly distant and isolated after his problems with women.

By this time, he rarely had a smile on his face and would visit his local bar, get blind drunk and glare at all the single females but not speak to any of them. He'd stopped shaving again and seemed to relish watching females react with horror to the unsightly tufts of hair sprouting out of his chin and cheeks. One local woman recalled: "He was a scary looking man with those weird fake teeth and facial hair. He looked creepy. He seemed deeply unhappy and often drank himself into a stupor. Then he'd end up insulting every woman in the bar before being thrown out."

Back at the fire station where he now worked, Dzhumag-aliev remained quiet and diligent most of the time. But then he announced to his colleagues that he was no longer willing to go into blazing buildings to save people. Dzhumagaliev insisted that it was too dangerous and that he wasn't prepared to sacrifice his life, despite his professional pledge as a fire fighter. Yet he somehow hung on to his job.

By the middle of 1978, Dzhumagaliev was living alone in a small cabin on the edge of town. One neighbour recalled of him: "He never said hello to anyone, so most of us avoided him whenever we could." Dzhumagaliev spent increasingly long periods out hunting alone for wild animals, includ-ing rabbits and deer, which he'd bring home, skin and eat. One man who accompanied him a few times into the local mountains recalled: "Dzhumagaliev was a very accomplished hunter. He didn't use a gun. He liked to wrestle animals to the ground and slit their throats with a knife. I asked him once why he didn't use a firearm and he said he preferred the feeling of overpowering an animal with his bare hands. He said guns were too easy. It was a strange remark. I brushed it off as being a bit eccentric but nothing more."

Dzhumagaliev's anger towards women continued to fester throughout the early winter of 1978. Even when he was out hunting, he couldn't get those feelings of resentment out of his head. Worse still, he began to wonder if he'd ever get married and have a family like most of his colleagues at the fire station.

This was when he committed that first killing of an innocent teenage girl.

* * *

The day after that first murder – 25 January 1979 – what little
remained of Dzhumagaliev's victim was found near the landfill site where he'd killed and dismembered her. A homicide
enquiry was launched by local police, but detectives were not
hopeful of solving it with no clear motive or obvious suspects.
At his nearby home, Nikolai Dzhumagaliev read in the local
newspaper about the discovery of the body as he feasted on yet
more of that same girl's remains. It had been just a couple of
days since the murder.

When Dzhumagaliev ran out of his first victim's meat a
few weeks later, he went out hunting again and killed another
young woman in chillingly similar circumstances to his first
victim. It was only when her remains were found a few days
after that murder in an isolated location near the town, in
a dismembered state, that detectives began to wonder if this
victim had been murdered by the same individual who'd
murdered the previous girl. But police didn't release any official details about this second killing as they didn't want to
cause panic among the local population.

They reacted similarly over the following eight months,
when Dzhumagaliev killed and ate at least five more women.
Each victim was raped before and after he killed them, which

qualified him as a full-blown necrophiliac. But little publicity was ever given to the murders and details about the victims remain scant to this day.

Dzhumagaliev later recalled that he particularly enjoyed the process of tracking each victim in the darkness, referring to it as "hunting down a woman". He attacked them all with either a knife or an axe before dismembering their bodies and taking flesh and body parts home in his backpack.

The only recognizable pattern noticed by the police at this stage was that the killer left a gap of approximately one month between each attack. Dzhumagaliev later said that was the time it took to eat each of his victims. He explained: "I'd look in the fridge and see there was no more meat, and then I knew it was time to go out hunting again."

Initially, Dzhumagaliev's victims following the first two were killed close to rivers and public parks. He'd track them through the darkness before pouncing in a secluded spot where he would speedily overpower them and drag them into nearby woodland. Then he forced two of them back to his own wooden cabin before raping and killing them and dumping their remains nearby. Dzhumagaliev continued turning his victims' less savoury meat into *pelemi* and is rumoured to have served human meat to unwitting friends at his home, although he later denied it.

As Dzhumagaliev stalked the region killing, raping and eating females, no one seemed to suspect that this strange, solitary man might be the monster who'd struck terror into an entire community. Yet there were elements of Dzhumagaliev's life and character that should have flagged him up as an obvious suspect. He was unmarried, had no children and lived alone with few friends. He was also well known in his neighbourhood for going out alone at night hunting "wild animals". Dzhumagaliev's psychopathic tendencies soon began to completely take over his life. With the killings, he'd unlocked something that had been lurking deep inside him for years.

Dzhumagaliev later claimed he was quite irritated that the police had completely failed to openly connect him to any of those early killings. Some experts have since speculated that he may have wanted to be caught and felt he was being encouraged to murder more women by the police's hopeless detective work.

At the fire station in the town where Dzhumagaliev was still working, his colleagues noticed he'd become even more withdrawn and less co-operative. One former colleague explained: "He kept snapping at any of us who dared to ask him what was wrong. He went into a complete shell. We actually thought he was having a nervous breakdown. Our fire chief was informed and recommended that Dzhumagaliev should be given some sick leave to give him a chance to recover."

On 21 August 1979 – after Dzhumagaliev heard he'd been reported to the chief of the fire department – he got blind drunk and attacked the colleague he suspected had informed on him. While they were scuffling, Dzhumagaliev produced a gun and shot his workmate dead.

Police who attended the scene of the killing had no idea that Dzhumagaliev was a mass murderer, so when they arrested him it was for the manslaughter of his fellow fireman. A few months afterwards, Dzhumagaliev appeared in court but was found not guilty by reason of insanity after he was diagnosed with schizophrenia following an examination by experts from Moscow's much-respected Serbsky Institute of Psychology.

Dzhumagaliev was greatly relieved by the court's decision as he would only have to stay a short time in a mental institution and the police still had no idea at the time that he'd murdered at least six innocent women. A year later, Dzhumagaliev was released and returned to his home town of Uzynagash.

He later claimed that the stay in the hospital had helped him to recharge his batteries and that he couldn't wait to get out and start killing women again. "I had a purpose in life," recalled Dzhumagaliev. "I still hated women and blamed them for most of my problems and by getting rid of some of them I felt I was doing all the men in the world a favour."

After his release, Dzhumangaliev managed to get himself a job as a labourer at a site near Almaty, which was close to his home town, Uzynagash. Within a couple of months, he'd killed two more women in fast succession. They provided Dzhumagaliev with plenty of fresh meat for his home-cooking sessions.

Then, on 1 December 1981, he bumped into a woman he knew in a local bar and persuaded her to accompany him to a hotel. He'd thought she wanted a genuine relationship, but when she rejected his advances, he killed her. While still in that hotel room, Dzhumagaliev decided to dismember her body to cover up his crime, as well as to provide him with some much-needed fresh meat.

The suite he was staying in was connected by a locked internal door to an adjoining room, where two other guests were staying. They'd heard the woman screaming a few moments earlier, followed by the sound of a man roaring like an animal. The two guests secretly watched Dzhumagaliev from their doorway as he left the room. They presumed he'd left for good, but in fact he'd gone out to get an axe so he could dismember the body of his latest victim. The two guests fled the hotel and immediately reported what they'd seen and heard to the police. Having got hold of an axe, Dzhumagaliev returned to the hotel room, stripped off all his clothes and began dismembering the woman's body, unaware that the police had been informed.

Minutes afterwards, an armed squad of detectives broke down the door to Dzhumagaliev's hotel room and found him – completely naked and covered in blood – calmly hacking at the woman's corpse lying on a table. The officers were so stunned by what they saw that they hesitated for a moment before trying to grab Dzhumagaliev. This hesitation meant he was able to escape down a fire ladder, still armed with that axe and with splatters of blood all over his naked body.

Dzhumagaliev jumped down from the bottom of the fire ladder onto an alleyway behind the hotel, before running naked onto the nearby high street through crowds of shoppers, knocking over two old ladies along the way. He then stole some clothes off a washing line and headed towards his cousin's home in the mountains that overlooked Uzynagash.

Some hours later, Dzhumagaliev found himself wandering along an isolated track while trying to keep away from main roads where he might be spotted. He was just about to enter a forest when he heard some rustling in nearby foliage. He immediately went into hunter mode – desperately hungry after so much time without food – by crouching down and then heading to where the noise came from.

Within a couple of minutes, Dzhumagaliev spotted a young woman walking alone through the greenery. Moments later, he pounced on her and strangled her and ripped out some of her innards to eat but left the rest of her "meat" behind because he had nothing to carry it in.

He eventually reached his cousin's house and was so exhausted by the journey that he fell asleep on a sofa within minutes of arriving.

The following day, Dzhumagaliev invited some of his cousin's friends round for a meal after bumping into one of them in the lane outside the house. None of them had any idea that he was on the run or that he'd just committed at least his eighth cold-blooded killing.

Shortly after they arrived, Dzhumagaliev persuaded one female guest to join him in the kitchen while he prepared the meal. When he tried to kiss her, she rejected him and Dzhumagaliev immediately killed her with a knife and gutted her body, covering himself with her blood. When two of his cousin's other friends walked into the kitchen, they found the severed head of their friend on a chopping board. Dzhumagaliev had her intestines in his hand.

Rather than fight a clearly unhinged man, the cousin's four friends fled the house and immediately reported what had happened to the police.

Officers who raided the house found Dzhumagaliev on his knees in the kitchen smeared with blood. He immediately confessed to murdering and eating women and told one detective: "I have this irresistible attraction to the female body. I wanted to know it fully and completely." Dzhumagaliev was handcuffed and taken to the nearest police station, where he agreed to be interviewed by detectives. Within minutes he'd admitted to murdering seven women.

On 3 December 1981, Dzhumagaliev was tried in court for murdering seven women between 1979 and 1981. Detectives and other experts suspected he had killed many more. Dzhumagaliev – who'd earlier been diagnosed with severe schizophrenia after killing his fireman colleague – was again declared insane and sent for eight years of compulsory treatment at a supposedly secure detention centre in the region of Tashkent.

Dzhumagaliev knew he'd been very lucky. Prosecutors were so unhappy about the relatively short sentence that they spent the following two years collecting evidence that proved Dzhumagaliev had killed at least double the seven victims he'd confessed to murdering. When these cases were proved, Dzhumagaliev's sentence inside that Tashkent mental facility was doubled to 16 years. But he was determined to avoid serving such a long sentence. Dzhumagaliev told other inmates he believed that his "specialized" hunting skills would help him escape, although it might take years of planning.

On 29 August 1989, Dzhumagaliev was being transported in a prison truck to another mental facility in Kyrgyzstan when he managed to overpower two guards and escape while the vehicle was stationary at traffic lights. Soviet law enforcement officials didn't inform the public that Dzhumagaliev was on the loose. They later claimed they'd wanted to avoid alarming the public.

Thus, Dzhumagaliev was left to wander around the USSR. Extraordinary claims later emerged that he committed more killings in the Moscow region where some of his family lived, as well as Kazakhstan. In fact, while on the run Dzhumagaliev headed straight for the nearest mountain range, just like his twelfth-century hero Genghis Khan would have done. He survived eating wild medicinal plants and drinking fresh water from streams and constantly kept on the move as authorities tried to track him down.

Dzhumagaliev ended up hiding out in those mountains for two years. He bartered for food with locals in a number of isolated villages. They had no idea he was a deadly psychopath on the run. Gradually, it became harder for him to stay hidden from police, though. After a report of a sighting of Dzhumagaliev, police recruited local citizens as lookouts and used hang-gliders to conduct aerial searches for him. One witness talked of a man matching Dzhumagaliev's description who was walking in fields on the side of a mountain. But by the time police reached the scene there was no sign of him. The whole time, though, the general public had no idea a mass murderer was on the run.

Dzhumagaliev eventually contacted a friend and convinced him to send a letter to those family members now living in the Moscow area. Dzhumagaliev wanted to give the authorities the impression that he'd headed to Russia's capital city. Dzhumagaliev's carefully constructed letter threatened to target more women in Moscow and stated that "nobody would miss them".

It wasn't until April 1991 that the citizens of Kazakhstan and the rest of what was now Russia learned that serial murderer Dzhumagaliev had been on the run for more than a year. And this was only after a Moscow newspaper published the inside story of Dzhumagaliev's escape, complete with unsubstantiated claims that he'd been seen in Moscow and the surrounding region, after a copy of his letter was passed to journalists.

Back in the mountains near Tashkent, Dzhumagaliev grew increasingly desperate. He contemplated returning to his home village but decided against that when he realized that a lot of residents would most likely turn him in to the police. Dzhumagaliev eventually decided to get himself arrested for a minor crime and sent to jail using a false identity. He believed prison was a better option than staying on the run in the wild and rugged mountains where he felt trapped and helpless.

So Dzhumagaliev stole half a dozen sheep from a field in Fergana, Uzbekistan, with the specific intention of making sure he'd be arrested and imprisoned in the Uzbek capital of Tashkent. But no one ever came after him.

In August 1991, Dzhumagaliev approached a woman on an isolated road near the town of Fergana, Uzbekistan and propositioned her. Within hours, the woman reported the incident to police. Investigators only took a few hours to track down Dzhumagaliev, who was arrested without incident after admitting he'd been out in the countryside looking for sheep to steal. Police had no idea who he really was.

Dzhumagaliev claimed he was a Chinese citizen, but he couldn't explain to police how and why he'd entered the Soviet Union. The Fergana officers became so suspicious that they requested help from law enforcement colleagues in Moscow because the man they'd arrested did seem to match the description of a wanted killer circulated to police stations across the region.

City detective Yuri Dubyagin travelled from the Russian capital to Fergana. Within minutes of arriving at the police station where Dzhumagaliev was detained, he recognized the arrested man. Dubyagin ordered that the prisoner be immediately dispatched under armed guard to a local mental hospital. Psychiatrists who examined Dzhumagaliev the following day declared him sane but insisted he should not have to face criminal charges until further tests had been carried out. They recommended that Dzhumagaliev should be sent to a more open clinic closer to his home town, Uzynagash.

When news of the impending transfer was leaked to residents of the town there was an angry backlash against the alleged homicidal maniac living near them, and the plan was immediately abandoned. Dzhumagaliev ended up being permanently detained at the hospital where he'd been sent following his arrest. But just a few months later, further psychiatric evaluation of him concluded that he was not a danger to anyone, despite his involvement in those previous murders. Within months, Dzhumagaliev was permitted to work as a repairman on day release from the clinic.

The reasons behind this prognosis and subsequent decision have never been properly explained by Russian law enforcement or mental health officials. One of Dzhumagaliev's doctors insisted to reporters at the time: "His behaviour is orderly, the patient is calm. He willingly works in the department, helping the staff. We have no grounds to say he is a danger to others. He can quietly be in society and be observed in a regular hospital."

The police were so outraged by the lenient treatment of Dzhumagaliev that they launched a cold case investigation into a number of Dzhumagaliev's other alleged killings. In September 2014, Dzhumagaliev was charged with the additional 1990 killing of a female student in Aktobe, western Kazakhstan. Her death featured all his usual trademarks. Dzhumagaliev was convicted and the court ordered that he should be re-detained in a secure mental hospital, near his old home town of Almaty.

Just over a year later – on 23 December 2015 – Dzhumagaliev escaped from that institution as well. Yet again, embarrassed law enforcement officials in the region refused to confirm or deny that Dzhumagaliev was once again on the run when news of the escape leaked to the local media. Instead, a police spokesman told reporters at the time: "We do not have information about the escape of the man and have no orders to catch him."

Many residents in Almaty – where Dzhumagaliev had once lived, as well as being close to the mental hospital he was now incarcerated in – had no doubt Dzhumagaliev was on the run. Some residents claimed they'd seen the confessed cannibal and killer walking on the streets of Almaty and his old home town, Uzynagash.

On New Year's Eve 2015 – just a week after Dzhumagaliev's latest alleged escape – a 22-year-old woman called Saida Akzhanova was murdered in a very similar fashion to the way Dzhumagaliev usually killed his victims. Local law enforcement still refused to publicly confirm whether or not Dzhumagaliev had escaped from that nearby mental hospital.

Over the following weeks, during January 2016, further rumours about Dzhumagaliev's escape appeared on WhatsApp and Facebook. Authorities still insisted Dzhumagaliev was in custody and released a statement allegedly from him in which he was quoted as claiming he'd had a complete change of heart when it came to the justice system. His statement said that he could no longer live with himself for having committed such heinous crimes and that he was intending to petition local prosecutors to ensure he was given the death penalty.

At the time of writing, this request has not been granted and there is still no concrete evidence that Dzhumagaliev really is back in custody. In 2019, rumours emerged in Almaty that Dzhumagaliev had been killed in a shoot-out with police when he was on the run. Typically, secretive law enforcement authorities refused to publicly confirm or deny the claims.

It's possible that Dzhumagaliev is hiding out in yet another isolated location. If that is true, then he is more than likely to still be killing in cold blood whenever his "appetite" demands it.

CHAPTER FIVE

DAMAGED BEYOND REPAIR

**Lasky, near Zhytomyr Oblast,
Soviet Territory of Ukraine, 25 July 1959**

Little Anatoly Onoprienko couldn't find his mother anywhere in their house. He kept shouting for her and ran from room to room but all to no avail. Then the four-year-old dashed into the back yard and headed towards the small shed where his mother sometimes went to have a cigarette after his father had been angry with her.

Onoprienko stopped just by the door to the shed and hesitated for a moment. He was worried what he might find in there. Finally, he gingerly opened the flimsy wooden door, walked in and stopped in his tracks. She was hanging by a rope from the ceiling.

The little boy looked up at his mother quizzically. He thought maybe she was playing a game, so he pushed her back and forth for a few moments and stepped back and watched her swinging. He even talked to her and asked her why she was hanging there, but she didn't reply.

Then his father Yuri walked in and shouted at the boy to leave as he pulled out a knife and slashed frantically at the rope she was hanging from. Onoprienko peeked back into the shed moments later and saw his father astride his mother thumping her chest and angrily howling like a monster over and over again. When he noticed his son watching him, he yelled at him to go away.

A few minutes later, Onoprienko was sitting at the kitchen table, still waiting for his mother to serve him some breakfast, when his father burst into the room.

"What did you do to her?" Yuri screamed at his small son over and over again. "What did you do to her?"

Onoprienko looked down, unsure how to react, and said nothing.

When his father stopped screaming at him, Onoprienko asked: "Why did mummy play those games? Why isn't she here now?"

Onoprienko's father smacked the back of his hand across the little boy's cheek so hard that he fell off the chair he was sitting on. When he tried to get up off the floor, his father kicked him in the pelvis. Then the boy was pulled roughly to his feet by his father, who then pressed his forehead hard against his son's head.

"Mummy's gone to heaven now."

"Why has she gone there?" asked the boy.

His father replied: "I will forgive you only if you go to my bed now and wait for me there."

Onoprienko recalled that he walked like a zombie up the stairs to the bed and got under the covers and waited for his father.

It was more than two years until local communist party officials in Lasky were informed by neighbours that they suspected Yuri Onoprienko had been abusing his young son both physically and sexually since before his mother died. They said he'd come back from the Second World War a damaged hero, who was deeply scarred by his experiences. One local resident – who'd known Onoprienko's mother since their school days together – later claimed she told her she'd decided to take her own life when she found out what her husband was doing to their son.

Party officials asked the dead mother's parents and sister if they'd take custody of the little boy to stop his father from abusing him, and they immediately agreed. Yuri only found out what was happening when his wife's parents and sister turned up at the house and said they were there to take the young Onoprienko. The father refused to let them in the front door. He then turned around and exploded at the little boy, accusing him of telling people about them. Onoprienko said he couldn't understand why his father was so angry with him. He didn't want to leave home. What his father had been doing to him had become a normal part of his life by this time.

Moments afterwards, the front door of the small, crumbling house flew open and Yuri Onoprienko dragged his seven-year-old younger son by his wrists down the wooden steps of the house in front of his wife's family members. He swung the little boy round by his wrists and threw him against a tree trunk in the front garden. The child collapsed sobbing on the ground.

From the front porch of the house, Onoprienko's grandparents and aunt stood shouting angrily at Yuri Onoprienko to stop while he stood over the child kicking him hard in the pelvis just like he'd done to the boy when his mother had died. The screams that followed were blood curdling. His mother's sister tried to grab Onoprienko's father to stop him, but he put her on the ground with one punch before continuing to kick his own son.

Eventually, Yuri stopped and looked down at the little boy shaking and curled up on the ground in a protective ball as if he was expecting more kicks at any moment. His father then turned around and stomped past the little boy's elderly grandparents and bloodied aunt to go back into his home, slamming the front door behind him. Incredibly, the police were never called to the scene.

That was one of the last times the boy ever saw his father. He was never able to express any hatred to or about his father. It actually became easier, Onoprienko said, to dislike his mother for having abandoned him four years earlier by killing herself. Later, Onoprienko would claim that her death was the most damaging memory he had of his childhood, rather than the beatings and abuse from his army veteran father.

The decision to take him away from the family home seemed like a form of rejection to the little boy. He'd kept his sick and warped father happy after suffering so much pain. He also absorbed the guilt they both felt by believing he'd been responsible for his own mother's death.

Within weeks of leaving the family home, Onoprienko's grandparents and aunt were struggling to control the damaged youngster. He was violent and destructive towards anything or anybody who got in his way, especially other children in the school playground or out on the streets, where he'd often disappear for hours on end.

On one particular day, Onoprienko secretly sneaked away from his grandparents' home to visit his father's house in the hope he could get him to allow him back. Onoprienko later said he was desperate to go home, where at least he felt needed. After he arrived at the house, Yuri beat his son savagely and dumped him, bruised and battered, back on the street. He didn't want him back because he didn't want the police involved in case he got arrested for child abuse.

The boy sat outside the house in the freezing cold for more than 12 hours in the hope that he would let him come back in, but he never did. When Onoprienko's grandparents showed up outside the house after being alerted by neighbours, they couldn't get the boy to leave. In the end, he had to be dragged into a taxi and driven back to his grandparents' home.

Less than a week after this incident, the anger Onoprienko had built up inside him led to him almost killing another child in a fight on the school playground. It was then that he was packed off to a state orphanage in the village of Pryvitne, in Volyn Oblast. Anatoly Onoprienko recalled that, after that, he felt as if everyone had abandoned him. Whenever he tried to contact his brother and father, they completely ignored him, and now his grandparents had left him as well. By the age of just eight, he was effectively all alone in the world.

The orphanage was a grim, strict establishment where discipline overrode all other priorities. Anatoly Onoprienko gave up on a lot of life after he got to that place. He later told one psychiatrist that the world hadn't shown him any care or loving, so why should he show it any in return? At an age when most children are blissfully ignorant of the world's problems, Onoprienko had already suffered more than most do in a lifetime. Little wonder he was seething with hatred for most of the human race.

He became so critical of himself, driven from a feeling of worthlessness that came from his abandonment, that it clouded his ability to evaluate his own life. He was lightning fast at misinterpreting other people's actions, which often meant he felt he was left with no option but to hurt them if they treated him badly. At the orphanage, teachers and other pupils quickly labelled him as "that troubled child". This made him feel even more isolated and "abnormal". While many children would retreat into a shell of self-doubt, Onoprienko's response was to hit back at anyone who stood in his way.

By the time he got to his mid-teens, Onoprienko's anger, combined with fury-triggering thoughts, were the only "tools" he used to help extinguish the pain he felt. Onoprienko later acknowledged that all this anger also helped him avoid dealing with the past. Hurting other people blocked out a lot of those memories. It gave him a purpose in life, and he was past caring what people thought of him anyway.

Animals were a different matter, though. When he shot a deer in the woods near his home for the first and only time, Onoprienko was reduced to tears by the sight of the animal lying dead in front of him. "I couldn't explain why I had done it, and I felt sorry for it. I never had that feeling again," he later recalled.

Onoprienko was thrown out of the orphanage at 15 and found himself having to fend for himself. Once again, he tried to contact his father and brother, but they'd moved house and were nowhere to be found. Onoprienko stayed in his home town of Lasky and survived on menial jobs, living in one room of a house belonging to a widow, for which he paid a very low rent. He had few friends and was extremely lonely, but at least he was in charge of his own destiny.

He decided to stay fit by joining a gym in a nearby village. In 1989, Onoprienko became friendly with a man called

Sergei Rogozin, at the same gym where they both worked out. It was one of the few times in his entire life that Onoprienko made friends with anyone. The two men began drinking together and swapped tales about their past. They both came from broken homes and hated their menial jobs, which paid just enough for them to get by.

One night, over far too many vodkas, Onoprienko and Rogozin agreed that they should start robbing houses to make some extra cash. They decided they'd target isolated properties in the countryside as they'd be less likely to be seen and would be able to escape more easily before the police arrived on the scene. The two friends also agreed they'd carry weapons for their own self-defence, just in case anyone tried to hurt them. Neither of them actually had a conversation about what they'd do if they were seen by any witnesses.

Their first raid involved breaking into a farmhouse near Lasky in early 1989. It did not go according to plan. The couple who owned the property confronted the two men the moment they got inside the property as their eight children slept upstairs. After a scuffle, the owner tried to hit the two men with a fire poker as they started heading up the stairs to the children. Within a matter of minutes, Onoprienko and Rogozin had killed the husband, his wife and all their children. They didn't want to leave anyone alive who could point them out to police.

Anatoly Onoprienko later claimed he felt bad about the killings and said that his friend Sergei had pressurized him into murdering the family in order to guarantee there would be no witnesses. Onoprienko did admit, though, to being very grateful for the extra cash he now had and said how he used it to have many more drunken nights out in bars. Only a few days after the raid, he and Sergei fell out when Onoprienko accused him of forcing them to kill the family. Whatever the truth of the matter, the two men went their separate ways, and that stolen money soon ran out.

It wasn't long before Onoprienko decided it was time to commit crimes on his own. At least he'd get to keep all the money for himself. He knew from that first raid that he'd be more likely to get away with committing robberies in isolated areas. So he headed out towards a small village some distance outside the city of Lasky. But on the way, he spotted a car parked up in an isolated layby. The windows of the vehicle were all steamed up and it was only when he got close to the car that he realized there was an entire family of five asleep in the vehicle.

Onoprienko banged on the windscreen, and when the man in the driver's seat opened his door, Onoprienko shot and killed him instantly. He then leaned inside the car at the screaming occupants and told them all to remain calm and he wouldn't hurt them. Then he leaned further into the vehicle and shot them all – including an 11-year-old boy – after deciding he wanted to ensure he got away with robbing them.

"I'd only approached the car to rob it," Onoprienko later recalled. "I was a completely different person back then. Had I known there were five people, I would have left." Onoprienko also insisted he'd derived no pleasure from the act of killing and claimed that having executed the family in cold blood, he got in the car and sat in stunned silence between the bodies of the two adults in the front bench seat. He waited until the point at which they began to smell. He later described the odour of the rotting corpses as being "unbearable", before adding: "Corpses are ugly. They stink and send out bad vibes."

Onoprienko eventually leaned across one of the bodies slumped next to him with the intention of opening the door and starting to remove the corpses from the car. But he kept changing his mind and stopping. For the following two hours, he remained in the front bench seat between those victims, unable to bring himself to deal with them.

Onoprienko later claimed that, as he sat there, he had flashbacks to his mother's corpse swinging back and forth, and to how angry his father had been when he found him in the shed that morning after she'd committed suicide.

Onoprienko eventually abandoned his plan to remove the corpses and instead clambered over the bodies, got out of the car and set fire to it. He stood back and watched as the flames engulfed the vehicle containing all the bodies.

* * *

A few days after this attack, Onoprienko selected another house in an isolated area near Lasky. This time he deliberately made a noise to attract the attention of its occupants so that someone would come out to investigate. Then he grabbed the house owner and forced him back into the property. Once inside, he killed the man and shot his spouse before rounding up their three children and murdering them. He stole all the cash he could find before setting fire to the property to destroy any clues that might help police find him.

Onoprienko had shot all his victims up this point, but on his next attack, also near Lasky, he took a knife. He went from room to room in that house stabbing the woman who lived there and her two sleeping children, including a three-month-old baby. He later claimed he didn't like wasting bullets on those too weak to resist him.

Unlike the majority of serial killers, Onoprienko did not sexually assault any of his victims. He insisted that his child-hood of pain and mental anguish at the hands of his father had been so brutal that the notion of forcing anyone to have sex in the way he had suffered was too much for his mind to bear. Onoprienko would claim he killed children because he was on a quest to save them from growing old and experiencing what he'd been through. He got revenge on every adult he came across after what they'd done to him in the past.

In the second half of 1989, Onoprienko raided at least three more isolated properties and killed more than a dozen people. He must have known he was starting to leave a trail for investigators, so he suddenly quit Ukraine. The police in Lasky had only just realized they had a mass killer on their hands, so his decision undoubtedly helped him avoid detection. And of course, once he'd gone, the killings in the region suddenly stopped. Detectives in Lasky couldn't hide their relief. After some months with no more murders, they put the files on each case away in a drawer presuming the killer had either died or been imprisoned for other crimes.

According to the Austrian and German authorities, Onoprienko spent some time from 1989 onwards committing crimes in both their countries. They have never officially disclosed what he did, except to confirm that he was deported back to Russia in 1995 after being arrested for burglary. Onoprienko has always insisted he worked as a manual labourer during much of the time he was in Europe. But many believe his main source of income came from burglaries and muggings. He has always claimed he did not commit any murders while travelling through Europe. Half a dozen other countries have since alleged that a man matching Onoprienko's description committed numerous other crimes, from break-ins to street robberies, though he was never arrested for any of these alleged offences.

Onoprienko later said that on his return to Ukraine from Europe in 1995, he was so determined not to go back to a life of crime that he moved away from his home region to live with a distant cousin in a town called Yavoriv in the hope he wouldn't be tempted to kill ever again. Yavoriv had once been home to a vast Soviet military base. But the recent fall of communism had led to the base being trimmed back in size. It was located close to Ukraine's border with Poland, in the heart of one of the most religious areas of the old Soviet Union.

While staying at his cousin's home in Yavoriv, Onoprienko met a woman called Anna, who had two children and lived in a flat very close to his home. Anna worked locally as a hairdresser and had been married to a serviceman, who knew Onoprienko's cousin as they'd served together at the local base. Onoprienko soon began a relationship with Anna, and this seems to have initially helped Onoprienko avoid returning to his murderous habits. Within months of meeting, he'd moved in with Anna and her children in her apartment.

But Onoprienko's dark, disturbing memories of his tormented childhood still haunted him. Just before Christmas 1995, Onoprienko found himself crashing into a deep depression, partly driven by the feeling that he wasn't able to return to his own relatives in Lasky to celebrate the festive season. Onoprienko became so bad-tempered that Anna ordered him out of the flat they were sharing, and he moved back in with his cousin.

Onoprienko later claimed that he felt very resentful after being rejected by Anna and that this provoked yet more disturbing childhood memories. On Christmas Eve 1995, Onoprienko broke into a secluded house belonging to the Zaichenko family, located in a village called Garmarnia, near the city of Yavoriv.

Onoprienko used a sawn-off double-barrelled shotgun he found at the house to murder the forestry teacher owner, along with his wife and two young sons. Onoprienko stole the couple's wedding rings, a small golden cross on a chain, earrings and a bundle of worn clothes. Before leaving the scene of his appalling crime, he set the property ablaze. Onoprienko blamed his decision to kill that family on his split with Anna. "I just shot them," he explained. "It's not that it gave me pleasure, but I felt this urge. I was upset." He added, in a detached voice: "From then on, it all became like some game from outer space."

Just over a week after this – on 2 January 1996 – Onoprienko shot and killed another family of four at their isolated home in the countryside near Yavoriv.

This time, though, while fleeing the scene, Onoprienko was seen by a man walking along the road in front of the house. Realizing he'd been spotted, Onoprienko made sure to kill the onlooker, in order to prevent any living witnesses from identifying him to the police. Onoprienko now found himself obliged to eliminate all witnesses, however far removed they were from the actual crimes he'd committed.

The day after those brutal, senseless murders, Onoprienko called round at girlfriend Anna's apartment loaded with some belated Christmas gifts for her children. Every item had been stolen from his most recent victims. Anna was so touched by his apparent generosity that she let him move back into the flat. Her children even began calling him "daddy". Unfortunately, being called daddy by those children triggered more of Onoprienko's childhood traumas, including flashbacks to the abuse he'd suffered at the hands of his own "daddy". The return to Anna's home would end up making Onoprienko even more anxious. He also now felt under enormous pressure to keep providing expensive gifts for her and her children.

On 6 January 1996 – just two days after returning to live at Anna's home – Onoprienko travelled to the nearby Berdyansk-Dnieprovskaya highway, where he'd decided he would stop cars and rob and kill the occupants. Onoprienko ended up shooting a naval cadet called Kasai, a taxi driver named Savitsky and a chief named Kochergina, as well as another unidentified motorist.

A few days after the slayings of those four innocent motorists, Onoprienko found himself back at home with Anna, having provided her and her children with yet more expensive gifts. Onoprienko recalled: "I remember I was sitting at home with Anna and her kids and I got this idea into my head that I may as well go out and kill more people since there was nothing else to do. I tried everything to push it out of my mind, but I couldn't."

On 17 January 1996, Onoprienko got in his car and once again headed out into the Russian wilderness. He eventually arrived on the outskirts of a small village called Bratkovichi and began prowling the narrow country lanes that encircled the community. Onoprienko later admitted he felt like an animal out looking for prey. "I needed to find something, anything, that I could kill," he said.

He found an isolated house owned by the Pilat family. Onoprienko recalled: "I sat and watched the house from my car like a wolf would stare at a sheep as he waited to pick the right moment to strike." When that perfect moment came, Onoprienko quietly got out of his car, broke into the house and shot all five family members, including a six-year-old boy. Then – having stolen everything of value that he could carry – he waited inside the property with the bodies until just before daybreak, when he set the house ablaze.

As Onoprienko got back into his car following the killings, he noticed two people in the distance walking along the main road. One was a 27-year-old female railroad worker. The other was her 56-year-old father. Onoprienko drove up to them on the deserted lane, rolled down his window and pretended to be lost. As they gave him directions, he calmly aimed his sawn-off shotgun at them through the window and blasted them both. Police who attended the scene said both of their faces had been literally blown to pieces. Afterwards, Onoprienko said he had felt no remorse at the time for shooting the pair of innocent bystanders. "I was in a deep void of darkness by this time. Nothing felt real."

He drove back home to Anna's flat loaded up with more toys and other presents for her and her children. That night – while Anna and her children slept – Onoprienko found himself pacing up and down in the apartment. He was tense and confused. He knew he'd just done something bad, but there was another side of him urging him to go out and do it all over again now.

Onoprienko tried to use vodka to knock himself out, so he could sleep off those disturbing feelings. However, the alcohol had the opposite effect and only fired up his desire to go out and find more people to kill. In attempting to explain his mind at the time, Onoprienko later said: "None of my victims had resisted. Armed or not, man or woman or child, none of them dared to do anything to stop me. Being a human being didn't mean anything to me anymore. All I could see were weak people. I compared humans to sand-grains. There were so many of them that they didn't mean a thing."

Onoprienko did eventually manage to shake off his demons that particular evening. But it didn't last long. Less than two weeks later – on 30 January 1996 – he drove to the town of Fastova, in the Kievskaya Oblast district. This time he broke into a house and killed a 28-year-old nurse, her two young sons and a 32-year-old male visitor.

Providing more gifts to Anna and her children was becoming tainted inside Onoprienko's head. He later said that while he'd enjoyed being appreciated by them, he also kept telling himself they were only being nice to him because he'd given them so many presents. By this time, Onoprienko had probably already killed 50 people.

On 19 February 1996, Onoprienko headed off to the nearby town of Olevsk, in the Zhitomirskaya Oblast district. Onoprienko broke into the home of the Dubchak family, where he shot the father and son and mauled the mother to death with a hammer, before turning his attention on the young daughter who'd witnessed it all.

She was kneeling and praying on the floor of her bedroom when Onoprienko walked in. She didn't look up at first.

"Where's the money?" asked Onoprienko.

The girl ignored him, closed her eyes tightly and continued praying.

"Show me where the fucking money is," he said flatly.

Onoprienko could see that her eyes were red from crying when she finally looked up. She still stared at him defiantly.

"No. I won't," she said quietly.

Onoprienko recalled: "Her strength was incredible. But I felt nothing, despite that." Onoprienko later claimed he felt both admiration and coldness at the same time. It was as if his mind was battling with itself to justify the murders, while at the same time acknowledging the full horror of his actions. Moments later, he shot the little girl, grabbed some of her toys and set fire to the house before heading off into the darkness once again.

On 27 February 1996, Onoprienko drove into the village of Malina, in the Lvivskaya Oblast district, and broke into the home of the Bodnarchuk family. He shot the husband and wife to death and murdered their two daughters, aged seven and eight. By this time, Onoprienko felt differently towards children, he later claimed. Now he wanted them to suffer like he had when he was young and innocent. He hacked both his latest child victims to death with an axe. He claimed he felt not an ounce of remorse.

The only children he didn't want to send to heaven were his girlfriend's as they were nice to him all the time. He convinced himself he was much gentler and kinder to them than their real father.

After hacking his latest child victims to death, Onoprienko was wiping the blood splatter off his face in the family bathroom when he heard the sound of someone else inside the house. A male neighbour had been alerted by the sound of gunshots, found the back door open and entered to see what had happened. Onoprienko shot and killed the man moments afterwards. Onoprienko was in such an over-hyped-up state by this time that he hacked at the corpse with the same axe he'd used to kill the two children earlier.

Onoprienko later tried to make sense of what he'd done. "Oh, you know, I killed them because I loved them so much, those children, the other man I had to kill. The inner voice spoke inside my mind and heart and pushed me so hard!" Detectives would say that "inner voice'" was nothing more than a chilling way to convince himself he had the right to kill.

A month later – on 22 March 1996 – Onoprienko travelled to the small village of Busk, just outside Bratkovichi, where he broke into a house and murdered all four members of the Novosad family. Once again, he took some toys and set fire to the house to eliminate any traces of evidence. Not surprisingly, the residents of Bratkovichi were terrified that their community had now been targeted twice by the same murderous monster.

The police had played a relatively low-key role up to this point. For reasons similar to those seen in other cases, they'd seemed unwilling to link all the killings, yet there was no denying that one man had been blowing the doors off homes on the edges of villages, gunning down adults and battering and stabbing children, as well as stealing money, jewellery, stereo equipment and other items before burning down each house. There was certainly a pattern.

But the second mass killing in the Bratkovichi area finally fired the authorities into action. The new nation of Ukraine dispatched a National Guard division, complete with armoured personnel carriers and a lethal array of weapons to protect the citizens of Bratkovichi and the surrounding districts where the killer had struck. In addition to that entire division of soldiers, more than 2,000 police investigators – both federal and local – were also drafted in to hunt for the killer, who was now suspected of murdering upwards of 50 people. Investigators still had no clear motive for the killings and, to make matters worse, they'd been committed in a catchment area populated by more than a million people. It was going to be incredibly hard to find whoever was responsible.

A few days after Onoprienko's latest attack, towards the end of March 1996, the Ukrainian Public Prosecutor's Office and its secretive Security Service of Ukraine (SBU) announced they'd arrested a suspect, who they were certain was the serial killer at the centre of the region's biggest ever manhunt. Yury Mozola, 26, had been caught by police loitering in one of the villages where Onoprienko had murdered an innocent family. Mozola ended up being tortured by six SBU investigators in front of a Public Prosecutor's Office representative for three days to get him to confess. His interrogation included beatings, burnings and even electric shock treatment. Mozola consistently denied all involvement with the murders and ended up dying after a long period of sustained torture. Despite the lack of confession, police immediately announced that he had been the serial killer they were hunting for and that now the good citizens of Ukraine could rest in peace.

Three days after this, Onoprienko raided an isolated farmhouse near the city of Odessa and killed the occupants. Not surprisingly, the public rapidly concluded that Mozola had not been the murderer after all. The Ukranian police had been humiliated. They'd poured huge resources into finding the killer and it had ended in abject failure. Worse still, their detectives were back at square one, it seemed. Many believed the only way police were going to catch this serial killer would be through a combination of good fortune and some very diligent on-the-ground detective work.

Police officer Oleg Khuney had worked his beat in Yavoriv – where Onoprienko was living with Anna and her two children – for 10 years and was regarded as a fine, diligent cop who really cared about his community. This included multiple estates of rundown, adobe-colored, five-storey residential housing complexes connected to the Soviet military base, which still dominated the town. Residents in these apartment blocks included serving and retired service personnel and their families. Officer Khuney was on first-name terms with many of the base's officers, and often mixed socially with them.

One of them was Onoprienko's cousin Pyotr Onoprienko, with whom Onoprienko had stayed when he first moved to the town. Army captain Pyotr lived with his wife and two children just 100 metres from Onoprienko's girlfriend Anna's apartment on Ivana Khristitelya Street. Pyotr had fallen out with his cousin after he had turned up on Pyotr's doorstep announcing that Anna had yet again kicked him out and that he wanted to stay with his cousin once more. Onoprienko became very threatening when Pyotr would only allow him to stay a few days while he found himself a new home. It was during this particular visit that Pyotr heard that Onoprienko's girlfriend had kicked him out this time after finding a cache of stolen weapons hidden in their home.

Pyotr asked his cousin to leave his home immediately. Onoprienko turned to Pyotr and said to his face: "God will punish you and your family." Pyotr was so worried about his wife and children's safety following his cousin's threat that Pyotr told his policeman friend Officer Khuney about Onoprienko and the stolen guns. He told Khuney he genuinely feared for his family's safety over the coming Easter holiday, even though Onoprienko had yet again persuaded his girlfriend to let him move back into her apartment after bringing more gifts for her and her children.

Pyotr mentioned all this to Khuney. He also said his cousin was from the Zhitomirskaya Oblast area, and the officer immediately remembered that this was the area where many of the earlier serial killings had occurred. Khuney located a police report about a 12-gauge, Russian-made Tos-34 hunting rifle – the type used in a recent local killing – which had been reported stolen in the Zhitomirskaya area. Officer Khuney recalled: "It was a long shot, but I thought, 'Here we've got an armed guy from the Zhitomirskaya Oblast, who had a weapon that matched the description of one missing. And we don't have too many people from that area come here.'"

Khuney called his bosses at Lviv Oblast police head-quarters for advice on how to proceed. Police chief General Bogdan Romanuk ordered his deputy, Sergie Kryukov, to assemble a task force in preparation for conducting a search of the apartment Anatoly Onoprienko shared with girlfriend Anna and her children. Romanuk also organized a team of local detectives and police to mount a huge manhunt in case Onoprienko wasn't in the apartment.

Before raiding the property on 16 April 1996, the police spent an hour in an identical third-floor corner apartment in a neighbouring block so they could study the layout. Other officers sealed the exits to the suspect's building with unmarked cars and sent two men each to guard the floors above and below their target's apartment.

With police and volunteers now in position around the entire building, Deputy Chief Kryukov, Officer Khuney and a patrolman colleague, Vladimir Kensalo, approached the apartment's front door and knocked. Onoprienko opened the front door almost immediately and didn't seem surprised to see them. He was so co-operative about being put in handcuffs that officers allowed him to keep his arms in front of him. He calmly explained that girlfriend Anna and her two children were at church, and that he was expecting them home at any moment.

Just after entering the apartment, Officer Khuney noticed an Akai tape deck in the sitting room. It was on a list of goods stolen from the Novosad family, who'd been murdered in the nearby area of Busk a few weeks earlier. As Khuney compared the deck's serial numbers with the list he was carrying, he noticed that Onoprienko now had a tense expression on his face. Khuney asked him for his identity card. Onoprienko led them to a closet, where he said he kept it. Khuney kept wondering why Onoprienko's expression had changed so suddenly moments earlier.

As Onoprienko leant into the closet to get his documents, he tried to grab a pistol from underneath some clothes. Having his hands in cuffs made the move difficult, though. Khuney forced him up against a wall and the weapon fell to the ground. Moments later, Khuney found a reference to the same pistol on the missing items list. It had been stolen from a recent murder scene near Odessa. Onoprienko was immediately escorted by three armed officers out of the apartment and down to a waiting police van.

Back in the apartment, other policemen recovered a total of 122 items belonging to Onoprienko's murder victims. This included a sawn-off Tos-34 shotgun missing from an earlier burglary, which had been used in the Bratkovichi and Busk killings and possibly other murders.

The officers were just winding up their search of the apartment when Onoprienko's girlfriend Anna arrived in her car outside the building and immediately noticed the police vehicles parked in front of the building. She sat in silence in the car for a few moments trying to gather her thoughts, having immediately suspected that the police were there for her boyfriend. When she eventually got out of her car outside the apartment block, Deputy Chief Kryukov approached. She asked him what was going on and explained who she was. He responded: "Do you remember those killings in Bratkovichi?" Onoprienko's girlfriend realized immediately what Kryukov was implying and broke down in tears. She said she had no idea what he'd done and had thought he was some kind of businessman.

At the police station, Deputy Chief Kryukov and his colleagues knew they still needed a full confession from their suspect, despite having recovered all those missing items taken from murder scenes. But Onoprienko's attempt to grab that gun and escape, plus his complete indifference towards the police, implied he was unlikely to admit he'd murdered dozens of innocent people. Kryukov confronted Onoprienko about the gun he'd tried to grab in the apartment, as well as some of the other items found there. Onoprienko smiled and said he would only talk to the officer heading up the investigation, before folding his arms, leaning back in his chair and refusing to say another word.

The city's lead investigator Bogdan Teslya was at home with his family watching television when he got a phone call from Kryukov asking him to come in and handle the interrogation. Teslya was a gregarious, dark-skinned man with a warm smile and a mouth full of gold teeth. He was considered by Kryukov, Khuney and many other officers to be their finest interrogator, thanks to his ability to speak calmly with criminals. He wasn't, however, the top-ranking police general that Onoprienko had demanded.

A few minutes before 10 p.m. on 16 April 1996 – following a second search of the apartment – Teslya walked into the police interview room and explained to Onoprienko that the general he'd requested had been held up. He would be there soon. Onoprienko had already waived his right to an attorney, so Teslya knew this was a unique opportunity to try and get as much information out of the suspect before he shut down.

"I was terrified that it would go wrong," Teslya recalled. "In this kind of case, you never know what will happen. He might have hung himself in his cell by the next morning, and then you'd never be able to properly close the case. We needed to get him to speak."

A few minutes later – at precisely 10 p.m. – Teslya ordered his colleagues to leave the interview room, and he repeated his explanation to Onoprienko about waiting for the general to arrive from Lviv. Teslya began making small talk while they continued to wait. Onoprienko's eyes narrowed and he refused to respond to any questions for the first half an hour as both men sat across the table from each other. Teslya kept talking anyway, despite Onoprienko's silence. He was trying to normalize the atmosphere in that interrogation room in the hope Onoprienko might eventually open up.

Then, after half an hour, Onoprienko sighed noisily, coughed and began talking about his own personal history. He told Teslya where he was born and how his mother had committed suicide when he was four years old and mentioned that his family had shipped him off to an orphanage in the Zhitomirskaya region. Teslya recalled: "Onoprienko said that he felt that his father could easily have taken care of him. He was visibly moved and got upset talking about it."

Onoprienko did not mention the child abuse allegations against his father.

Teslya asked Onoprienko whether he ever felt resentment toward families as a result of what he'd suffered. Onoprienko hesitated briefly and shook his head before restating that he would not talk to anyone below the rank of general. Teslya had clearly hit a nerve. So Teslya tried a different approach.

"We'll get you your generals," he told Onoprienko. "We'll get 10 generals if you want. But how am I going to look if I bring them in here and you've got nothing to tell them? Because maybe there's nothing to tell. How will I look then?"

Onoprienko's eyes narrowed again as he thought about what Teslya had said. He slowly began nodding to himself.

"Don't worry. There's definitely something to tell."

By this time, it was about 11:30 p.m. Teslya left the room and went into the corridor, where General Bogdan Romanuk – who'd actually arrived more than an hour earlier – was waiting. After a five-minute briefing from Teslya, the two men and the general's personal assistant, Maryan Pleyukh, entered the interview room. Onoprienko beamed when he saw the general, and that's when the police concluded that one of his motives for killing so many innocent people had been the need to "be someone".

Then Onoprienko began his full confession. He started by admitting he'd stolen the shotgun, and that he'd used it in a recent murder. He described how he'd shot that family to death and set their home ablaze in order to destroy any evidence.

Onoprienko paused and his voice softened. "I'm not a maniac," he insisted. "If I were, I would have thrown myself onto you and killed you right here. No, it's just not that simple. I've been taken over by a higher force, something telepathic or cosmic, which drove me to do all this. I'm like a rabbit in a laboratory. A part of an experiment to prove that man is capable of murdering and learning to live with his crimes. To show that I can cope, that I can stand anything, forget everything."

Onoprienko began sobbing. The three men sat with Onoprienko right through the night until 6 a.m. as he confessed to a total of 52 murders.

Each killing had to be carefully written up, so it was a slow process. Officer Teslya later observed: "When he talked about the reasons for the killings, he completely lost his resemblance to a rational person." Onoprienko kept describing himself to police as a "hostage". He urged the police to track down the unknown force that drove him to kill in the first place. Onoprienko then switched tacks and admitted he was relishing the attention of the media, which seemed to suggest that he really did enjoy the fame. And all three interrogators noticed that Onoprienko offered them virtually no motive for the murders. He kept repeating that he considered himself to be a "phenomenon of nature" who had been commanded "from above" to kill.

After that first interview session ended, Onoprienko was taken in a police truck to a detention centre on the outskirts of Lviv. The following morning, Officer Teslya began a five-day series of one-on-one interviews with Onoprienko. He described the suspect as "the most perplexing person I've ever interviewed".

Teslya recalled that it felt as if he was on a roller-coaster ride, during which he struggled to keep track of Onoprienko's dual personalities amid a sea of grisly revelations. On one side was a rational, educated, eloquent young man. On the other was a deranged, homicidal megalomaniac. Teslya explained: "In Onoprienko's case, no matter how long I spent with him, I was still left with two completely contradictory views of his personality."

At one stage, Onoprienko claimed he could exert strong hypnotic powers, control animals through telepathy and stop his heart with his mind through his mastery of yoga. Teslya deliberately feigned being impressed by his suspect's "hidden powers".

"That sounds fascinating," he told Onoprienko. "Perhaps for my benefit, you could try them on me."

Onoprienko looked confused by the police officer's willingness to engage on such matters.

"Yes but it only works with weak people, and you aren't a weak enough person," responded Onoprienko.

On Friday 19 April, Teslya was officially instructed to hand over the case to Ukraine's federal Interior Ministry investigators. Teslya had no doubt that Onoprienko was genuinely insane and that he had acted alone. Teslya explained: "There have been many rumours that he was part of a gang, but my feeling was that his discussions of his motives, and of his special powers, were not fabricated. I could be wrong, but that's what I think. Plus, just thinking rationally, I don't think anyone but a single killer could have pulled off so many murders. In a gang, someone talks, another drinks, a third whispers something to a girlfriend, and it's all over. You'd never make it to 52 killings. But as I said, I could be wrong."

But many people in the Lviv area – including the killer's cousin Pyotr Onoprienko – insisted they still feared for their lives on the basis that Anatoly Onoprienko had people "standing behind him".

Psychiatrists declared Anatoly Onoprienko mentally fit to stand trial. The actual proceedings did not begin until November 1998 – more than two years after the arrest – because criminal trials in the new Ukraine could not begin until a defendant had read all the evidence against them. In the case of Anatoly Onoprienko, there was a mountain of paperwork plus 99 volumes of gruesome photos, showing dismembered bodies, cars, houses and random objects that Onoprienko had stolen from his many victims. Another reason for the delay was financial. Chief judge Dmitry Lipsky had to make a televised appeal to put pressure on the Ukrainian government to allocate the necessary funds for such a lengthy trial.

Onoprienko's trial eventually opened in the city of Zhytomyr, 90 miles west of the capital Kiev on 12 February 1999.
As the proceedings began, Onoprienko – like notorious Rostov
serial killer Andrei Chikatilo – sat in court in a metal cage, and
was spat upon and raged at by the public. Afraid that someone
might take the law into their own hands, police searched bags
and made everyone pass through an airport-style metal detector
before entering the court each day. Dozens of people huddled
together in the public gallery of the unheated courtroom, glaring constantly down at Onoprienko in the dock. "Let us tear
him apart," one woman shouted from the back of the court
room just before the hearing started. "He does not deserve to
be shot. He needs to die a slow and agonizing death."

Prosecutor Yury Ignatenko maintained in court that the
key to Onoprienko's motives lay in his own violent nature.
Ignatenko told the court: "In every society there have been
and are people who due to their innate natures can kill, and
then there are those who will never do that. People may well
ask how come he killed so many people. But why not, if
conditions make that possible? Onoprienko led a double life,
and that is the key to how he was able to murder so many and
yet lead an otherwise apparently normal life."

When Judge Dmitry Lipsky asked Onoprienko if he
would like to make a statement, he replied with a shrug of
his shoulders. "No, nothing," he whispered. Then – informed
of his legal right to object to the court's proceedings – he

growled: "This is your law. I consider myself a hostage." Asked to state his nationality, Onoprienko said: "None." When Judge Lipsky said this was impossible, Onoprienko rolled his eyes and replied: "Well, according to law enforcement officers, I'm Ukrainian."

"I perceive it all as a kind of experiment," Onoprienko later said of the supposed conspiracies against him. "There can be no answer in this experiment to what you're trying to learn."

One criminologist explained: "The only voices in his head were his own. He'd had that inner self ordering him about since the day he was taken from his family." Onoprienko went on to tell the court he felt like a robot driven for years by a dark force and repeated his earlier claim that he should not be tried until authorities could determine the source.

"You are not able to take me as I am," Onoprienko shouted at Judge Lipsky. "You do not see all the good I am going to do, and you will never understand me. You will never understand this. Maybe only your grandchildren will understand." Onoprienko looked away and took a long, deep breath before turning back to the judge again. "I would kill today in spite of anything," he told the judge and the rest of the hushed court. "Today I am a beast of Satan."

Onoprienko said nothing more in court. His lawyer Ruslan Moshkovsky did not contest his client's guilt. Instead, he blamed the ineptitude of police investigators for not catching him earlier, which could have saved dozens of victims.

Closing arguments began in early April 1999. Many of those attending the hearing feared that the killer would be sentenced to only 15 years in prison – the maximum sentence possible under Ukrainian law outside of capital punishment. Prosecutor Yury Ignatenko wasted little time in demanding a death sentence. "In view of the extreme danger posed by Onoprienko as a person, I consider that the punishment for him must also be extreme – in the form of the death sentence."

Onoprienko's lawyer Moshkovsky played up the miserable childhood of his client in his closing arguments. "My defendant was from the age of four deprived of motherly love, and the absence of care, which is necessary for the formation of a real man," Moshkovsky said. "I appeal to the court … to soften the punishment."

The trial was adjourned to await the judge's final verdict. Three hours later, Judge Lipsky returned to the court and announced the verdict was ready to be given. Onoprienko stood up and stared down at the floor of his metal cage as the judge said "guilty". Judge Lipsky told him: "In line with Ukraine's criminal code, you are sentenced to the death penalty by shooting." Onoprienko's co-defendant Sergei Rogozin, accused of helping in the first set of murders, was sentenced to just 13 years in prison.

Afterwards, Onoprienko issued a statement through his lawyer: "I've robbed and killed, but I'm a robot, I don't feel anything, I've been close to death so many times that it's interesting for me now to venture into the afterworld, to see what is there, after this death."

But the drama and fallout from the Onoprienko case was far from over.

The judge's death sentence ruling put the Ukrainian authorities in an awkward position. As a new Council of Europe member, they were obliged to commit to abolishing capital punishment. But both the public and politicians across the country wanted Onoprienko to be executed, due to the enormity of his crimes.

Following the sentencing, Onoprienko gave a lengthy interview to the Russian correspondent for the UK newspaper *The Times*. During their meeting, Onoprienko reminisced almost fondly about the murders he'd committed. "To me killing people is like ripping up a duvet … Men, women, old people, children, they are all the same. I have never felt sorry for those I killed. No love, no hatred, just blind indifference. I don't see them as individuals, but just as masses.

"If I am ever let out, I will start killing again, but this time it will be worse,10 times worse. The urge is there. Seize this chance because I am being groomed to serve Satan. After what I have learnt out there, I have no competitors in my field. And if I am not killed, I will escape from this jail and the first thing I'll do is find Kuchma [the Ukrainian president] and hang him from a tree by his testicles."

Onoprienko also told the reporter: "I started preparing for prison life a long time ago – I fasted, did yoga, I am not afraid of death. Death for me is nothing. Naturally, I would prefer the death penalty. I have absolutely no interest in relations with people. I have betrayed them."

Onoprienko claimed he'd been shaken by people's cowardice while committing his crimes. He said that when slaughtering one family in a village, no one came to help them, even though neighbours must have heard the victims' screams. "Everybody went into hiding, like mice," said Onoprienko.

One of the detectives involved in Onoprienko's original arrest recalled having been shocked at how easily the mass killer had managed to manipulate the court into giving him a death sentence. "He was mad. I have no doubt about it," said the detective. "That means his evidence should have been treated as such but instead the court and the authorities played into the popular opinion, which clearly said he must die for his crimes. That was exactly what he wanted, so in effect he won."

Anatoly Onoprienko continued to reside on death row as Ukrainian authorities pushed for his death sentence by launching a new multiple-murder probe to tie him to further killings, in addition to the ones he'd already confessed to. Investigators this time concentrated on the period between 1989 and 1995, when Onoprienko had spent much of his time elsewhere in Europe.

Meanwhile, Onoprienko gave another reporter an interview. He said: "I've never regretted anything and I don't regret anything now. I love all people and I loved those I killed. I looked those children I murdered in the eyes and knew that it had to be done." He claimed in the same interview that he would have been prepared to kill his own son, if he'd had one. The question of Onoprienko's execution dominated the media.

Onoprienko never got his wish of being executed. On 27 August 2013, he succumbed to heart failure and died of natural causes in the Zhytomyr prison where he'd been incarcerated. He was 54 years old.

Today, experts have a phrase to describe the pain he suffered as a child. It is known as "second-hand emotion" because the anger that he first felt when he was four years old provided the spark that triggered all of his chilling crimes.

Onoprienko once compared himself to Mikhail Bulgakov, one of Russia's darkest authors. Onoprienko said just before he died: "I feel related with Messir, the hero from one of the Bulgakov's book. He was evil, and so am I. I did what I had to do: kill people. I don't owe any more explanation to my victims, their families and the police."

CHAPTER SIX

LINE OF DUTY

Angarsk, eastern Russia, December 1998

Teenage schoolgirl Svetlana Misyavitchus hated walking home
from her best friend's house at night, but she had little choice
in the matter as no one in her family owned a car. On this
particularly cold evening, dense snow was falling, and she
could barely see more than 50 yards in front of her. The streets
of Angarsk were eerily empty because few people in these parts
ventured out after darkness fell, especially in such extreme
weather conditions.

It was a neighbourhood where blocks of apartments dominated sprawling concrete housing estates that overlooked huge
factories, many of which had thick poisonous clouds belch-
ing out of them day and night. To make matters worse for
17-year-old Svetlana, most of the street lights on her route
home had either been broken by vandals or simply allowed to
burn out to save money. Times were hard in this former Soviet

enclave back in 1998. Local authorities were often broke and the country's infrastructure since the fall of communism at the start of the decade had been crumbling at an alarming rate.

Svetlana was just about to cross a deserted, windswept road when she noticed a car turn into the street about two hundred metres ahead of her. At first, she stopped in her tracks, scared that it might mean trouble. A lot of men kerb-crawled around the nearby industrial estate at night looking for women to pay for sex. When the weather was as bad as it was that evening, they often looked further afield for prostitutes because so few were out in their usual haunts. Over the previous few months, Svetlana had twice angrily rejected male motorists who'd offered her cash and tried to persuade her to get in their cars. Luckily, neither of the men had got violent with her. Svetlana had two school friends who'd not been so fortunate and had almost ended up being raped in recent months.

Svetlana took a short, sharp intake of breath and continued to walk across the street, even though the car she'd just seen was moving slowly in her direction. As she always did when these sorts of situations arose, Svetlana stared down at the pavement and kept walking. Her mother had told her long ago that she shouldn't look these sorts of men in the eye as that would only encourage them.

It was only as she reached the other side of the street that Svetlana sneaked another glance at the vehicle and realized it was a police cruiser. She felt much safer, so she lifted her head, held her shoulders back and continued walking on the pavement that bordered an abandoned warehouse with cracked and smashed, smoke-burnt glass windows. Svetlana noticed out of the corner of her eye that there was only one cop in the car, which was unusual as they tended to work in pairs. But she didn't give it much thought and continued her journey.

The snow started falling even harder moments later, muffling the sound of the police car's engine. Svetlana turned for a brief moment and looked behind her. It was only then that she realized the vehicle was very close to her, no more than 15 metres away. She quickened her pace and nearly lost her balance on a slippery cracked slab of pavement. As a strong northerly wind picked up, sheets of snow swept across the road.

Behind her, she heard the police cruiser's engine revving. It pulled up alongside her. Svetlana looked across just as the uniformed driver wound down his window and smiled. She stopped. The snowfall had turned into a full-blown blizzard by this time, so it was hard for her to see him clearly. He was a policeman and he was quite old, so that made her feel safer.

The officer asked her in a fatherly manner why she was out so late. She told him the truth, that she was on her way home after a visit to a friend's house.

He had a gentle, relaxed, laid-back voice, which immediately put her at her ease. He asked her where she lived. She hesitated for a moment and answered. When he offered her a ride home, she shivered from the cold and wet and nodded. After all, he was a policeman.

Svetlana headed towards the front passenger side of the car, but he told her to get in the back. After climbing in, the car moved off. She noticed his dark eyes watching her in his rear-view mirror and tried to smile up at him. There was very little conversation between them. Svetlana was shy and felt awkward being in a car with an older man, although at least he was a police officer. In any case, there was a wire mesh between them, although she didn't mind because it made her feel safer. The cop was just as quiet. Svetlana glanced down at the floor, so that she didn't have to look at his eyes constantly watching her in the rear-view mirror. At least she knew she'd be home in a couple of minutes.

As the cruiser turned into Svetlana's street, she felt relieved. She didn't know why, since the officer had been extremely polite and respectful throughout the journey. The blizzard continued sweeping thick, spongy dollops of snow across the street and the squeaky windscreen wipers were struggling to cope.

As they approached her apartment block, she held tightly onto her bag in anticipation that they were about to stop and told him her home was just ahead. She was about to grasp the door handle to leave the car when she noticed it hadn't slowed down. She repeated that her block of flats was just ahead. He didn't answer. The car picked up speed. She looked up at the rear-view mirror. He wasn't watching her now. His eyes had narrowed and he was looking straight ahead.

"What are you doing?" she asked. He didn't answer. She pulled at the door handle just as they passed the front entrance to her apartment block, but it wouldn't open. She couldn't even open the window, either. Svetlana screamed as loudly as she could in the hope that someone might hear her. The street was deserted and there were few lights on inside the overlooking apartments.

As the car swung across the road and turned down a narrow track alongside a high factory fence topped with barbed wire, Svetlana began clawing at the mesh barrier between them. He was grasping the steering wheel tightly and didn't look behind at her once.

The police car eventually shuddered to a halt on a darkened, deserted stretch of wasteland. Svetlana was still screaming and clawing hysterically at the mesh fence between her and the policeman. He got out of the car and ripped open the back door and dragged her by the hair out onto the frozen ground. Then he climbed on top of her and unzipped his trousers. She tried to wriggle beneath him, so he started choking her with his right hand while he guided himself inside her. He didn't utter a word throughout the assault.

Svetlana decided it was safer not to put up a fight and went limp beneath him. When he'd finished, he got up, took a cosh out of his holster and stood over her for a few moments smacking it in the palm of his hand over and over again as she sobbed. He leaned down and smashed it over the top of her head with such ferocity that she was instantly knocked unconscious.

Svetlana eventually opened her eyes to find him repeatedly banging her head against a tree. She was almost completely naked. Then she crumpled to the ground. "Why are you doing this?" she screamed at him. "Why? Why? Why?" He said nothing as he clutched her neck and lifted her up again and continued smashing her head over and over against the same tree trunk. Svetlana shook uncontrollably throughout the relentless assault, which seemed to her to be endless.

Eventually, he let go and she once again crumpled to the frozen ground beneath the tree trunk. In that brief moment, Svetlana tried to scramble out from under him on all fours, but he stamped hard on her back and she collapsed to the ground again. This time he began kicking her along the frozen surface like a human football until they reached the top of some rickety, makeshift wooden steps. Then he pushed his boot so hard into her back that she rolled down them.

At the bottom, he raped her again but still said nothing. After he'd finished, he got off her and stood over her, hands on hips like he had before. She wanted to cry but instead she kept her eyes tightly shut and played dead. She felt his breath close to her face as he leaned down to examine her to see if she was still alive.

The sound of breaking twigs and snow crunching underfoot suddenly distracted him. He crouched silently as he stopped to listen to the noise of someone walking nearby in the forest. When everything went quiet once again, he got up, brushed himself down and walked off into the shadows towards his police car. Svetlana opened her eyes just wide enough to see him get into the vehicle. She heard the engine start up and watched as it moved off.

As she struggled to her feet, she heard more sounds of twigs cracking and snow crunching in the nearby freezing darkness. Svetlana looked up as steam from someone's breath drifted across a moonlit bush nearby. She could just make out the silhouette of an elderly man with a walking stick and his dog. She shouted for help as she tried with difficulty to get up from the freezing snow, virtually naked. Moments afterwards, the old man appeared in front of her. He looked down at her, spat on her and called her a whore before walking off with his dog. He'd come across many prostitutes in those woods over the years and felt nothing but disgust for all of them.

Svetlana sobbed as she finally struggled to her feet and managed to retrieve some of the torn shreds of her clothes scattered across the snowy ground. She found her ripped coat and put it on, even though one of the arms was missing. Then she heard the sound of a car in the distance from the nearby main road and stumbled through the dense woodland snow to where it was coming from.

When she got to the road, she tried to tidy herself up. She looked up as the headlights came into view in the distance. As the vehicle got closer, she began waving it down. Its full beams were so strong that she couldn't make out the shape of the car. She stepped out further into the road, almost slipping on the icy tarmac to make sure she was seen. The vehicle didn't slow down, so she frantically waved and shouted as it got closer and closer.

Moments later, the wing of the vehicle clipped Svetlana as she tried to dive out of its way. It knocked her backwards into the snowy bank. As she tried to get back on her feet, the shadowy outline of a man stood over her. It was only then she realized it was the same policeman who'd just raped her.

As he undid his trousers, Svetlana's entire life flashed before her. When would this living nightmare end? If he'd come back to kill her, she just wished he would do it now and put her out of her agony. That was when she lost consciousness again.

* * *

The next thing Svetlana remembered was waking up and there being someone looking down at her. She shivered with fear and shut her eyes tight again immediately, presuming that she was still in the woodland and that the man was about to assault her yet again.

The icy temperature felt different from the forest, though, so she opened her eyes just enough to see that the person standing next to her was not the policeman but a man in a white coat. He lifted her limp arm and started to examine her fingernails. Svetlana could just make out through her slightly open eyes a toe with a tag on it next to her. Then she realized it was a corpse lying on a trolley.

Svetlana screamed and the man in the white coat dropped his instrument to the floor and shouted for help, while opening her eyes and feeling for a pulse. She'd been taken to the hospital morgue after paramedics had wrongly pronounced her dead after recovering her body from the side of the road.

Svetlana was so traumatized that for the following 24 hours she could not even tell doctors her name or age. Half of her hair had been pulled out from her scalp and the rest of it had turned grey. She'd been paralyzed down one entire side of her body, suffering so much brain damage she could barely move or talk.

Svetlana had been a virgin before the attack occurred. Rape and near death had been her first sexual experience. Later she would find out he'd given her syphilis. And in the middle of all this trauma, Svetlana and her family waited for the police to investigate. At first, no one bothered to visit her. When her mother complained, a young male officer eventually turned up at the hospital. He seemed indifferent to the attack and presumed she was a local prostitute whose customer had "turned nasty".

Svetlana dutifully provided the stern-looking detective with details of every moment she could recall, including the rape, her assailant's police uniform, his car and the exact time the attack had happened. The officer seemed unsurprised by the allegation that the attacker was one of his colleagues. It wasn't until 24 hours afterwards that he returned to her bedside with a photo of a 54-year-old officer called Mikael Popkov, who'd been on patrol in the area on the night in question.

Svetlana immediately identified him as her attacker. She also confirmed details about the inside of his car. The detective interviewing her seemed far from convinced, though. He insisted that the cop's own wife – also a police officer – had already provided Popkov with an airtight alibi. She'd even told a detective that he was the perfect husband and father to their children. Despite protests from Svetlana and her mother, the rape investigation was quickly shelved.

Popkov was fortunate that he hadn't killed Svetlana, even though that had undoubtedly been his intention. One detective later admitted that if police had had to launch a murder enquiry, then they would have been more diligent about linking the attack to earlier murders. Assaults on women were not given much priority inside the city's hard-pressed police service at the time.

Popkov later admitted that he regularly fantasized about what he'd done to Svetlana and other women. But he said that in the end he would grow bored of reliving each attack inside his head and would then decide to go out and find a new target.

* * *

Mikael Popkov had joined the police back in the mid-1980s before the fall of the Soviet Union, so he was very much part of the mindset of the previous communist regime. Back then the police were viewed with suspicion by the public. They were feared by many who were convinced they would shoot first and ask questions later.

Popkov met his wife Elena – also an officer – after joining the police, and they'd married when he was 22 and she was 20. They were both considered diligent officers. Two years after the marriage, Elena gave birth to a daughter, Ekaterina. Popkov was extremely possessive, jealous and controlling. Friends of the couple recalled that, soon after their marriage in 1986, Mikhail Popkov spoke about wanting to put his new wife under surveillance to make sure she was not cheating on him. Other friends said that Popkov had a vicious temper and would fly into fits of rage at the mention of any women he deemed to be promiscuous.

In late 1987, three local women came forward and reported to police that they'd rejected Popkov's offer of a ride home. That should have been clear evidence that Popkov was out prowling the streets for women, but most of his colleagues refused to believe he was involved in any such nefarious activities. Popkov was warned by one colleague that he was being "kept an eye on", and as a result he resisted his urges and managed to avoid any more incidents.

Then, in the late summer of 1992, Popkov came home to find his wife Elena in the company of one of their colleagues,

Alexey Mulyavin. The two of them were alone in his house. Even though Elena and her friend were not doing anything, Popkov exploded and accused Elena of having an affair. She denied it venomously. The following morning, he fished two used condoms out of the trash can at the family home and threw them on the table in front of his wife as further evidence that she had cheated. Later it emerged that the condoms had been used by a couple who were staying with the Popkovs as guests.

At home and at work, Popkov began openly talking in a negative fashion about women who went out at night to drink without their husbands or boyfriends. Years later he admitted: "I had no right to evaluate people, their behaviour … this is my repentance." But at the time of his wife's alleged extra-marital relationship in the summer of 1992, Popkov became so bitter that he went and had an affair of his own, although he never admitted who it was with or exactly when it occurred. He claimed he thought it would quell his anger, but he later admitted it made him more dangerous, as he then felt guilty about his own behaviour.

Then one night in December 1992, his wife finally admitted that she'd cheated on him, and he realized that all his suspicions had been true after all. Popkov became so angry that he decided to kill his wife there and then, but their daughter walked into the room. Instead, he went out looking for women to punish.

He began waiting outside clubs and restaurants, where he'd watch single women leaving and pull up beside them as they walked home, offering them a lift or suggesting they go for a drink together. Sometimes he'd even threaten to arrest them if they refused to get in. Then he'd drive his victims to the edge of woods and forests and drag them out of the vehicle. They would then be beaten, sexually assaulted, strangled, struck with blunt objects and, if they hadn't died by then, he would sometimes stab them repeatedly.

Popkov later claimed that while killing his victims, he would often flash back to visions of his childhood when his mother had disgusted him with her behaviour. This further compounded his conviction that all women were disgusting and debauched and needed to be taken out.

Popkov recalled: "The choice of weapons for my early killings was always casual. I never prepared beforehand to commit a murder, I could use any object that was in the car – a knife, an axe, a bat." Popkov decided from the beginning of his reign of terror that none of his victims would survive, so he could "clean up" the streets. After each murder, Popkov returned home to his family as if nothing happened.

Murder squad detectives were unable to comprehend that there was a possible serial killer in their midst. As a result, the first half-dozen murders weren't officially connected to each other by investigators. Popkov became so brazen that sometimes he actually entered nightclubs and restaurants in his police uniform, even while he was off duty. This no doubt helped him further convince his would-be victims that it would be "safe" for them to accept his offer of a ride home in his police cruiser.

He also began using confiscated items from other crime scenes as his murder weapons – replacing them at the original crime scene when he was done.

On other occasions, Popkov stole items from his police department's store of confiscated weapons. He'd throw them away near the crime scene after wiping them carefully to remove his fingerprints.

Even after witnesses began telling police that some victims had been seen talking to a police officer shortly before they disappeared, detectives failed to acknowledge that a police officer might be responsible for the murders. Some officers implied that the victims had been loose women, who deserved what they got.

Popkov's attacks contained classic, regular patterns. His victims were all murdered in or close to where he lived, Angarsk. He used similar weapons: namely, an axe, a hammer or sometimes a screwdriver. But detectives were confused by some of his other tactics that were less consistent, including one occasion when he carved the heart out of a woman and another when he beheaded his victim. Sometimes, he even ended his attack by hanging them in a noose. Bodies were also found in strange poses because he raped them in abnormal ways. They'd be dumped in forests, by the roadside or in a local cemetery.

By 1995 – despite the denials of the police – the media in Angarsk and the general public began to suggest that a serial killer must be at large. But the ever-stubborn city police claimed that each murder was part of a territorial war connected to gangs running drugs and prostitution rackets. They insisted these criminals were deliberately trying to dress up the murders as the work of one deranged killer.

In 1996, Officer Popkov shot dead a rapist during an arrest. Some detectives later concluded that Popkov deliberately killed the man in the hope that he'd get the blame for some of his own attacks. There was an internal investigation into the incident, and Popkov was cleared after his bosses backed up his decision to shoot the rapist as he'd allegedly tried to take two other officers hostage and escape. But detectives concluded, much to Popkov's irritation, that the man had not been connected to the murders he'd committed.

As the deaths piled up, most of Popkov's work colleagues continued to consider him to be a morally upstanding, amusing character who was always the life and soul of any party. In the summer of 1997, he was promoted to second lieutenant in the Angarsk city police force. But, privately, he'd given himself the title of "the cleaner", as he believed his most important mission was to take "filthy women" off the streets.

* * *

On 29 October 1998, Popkov attacked and murdered married mother-of-one Tatiana (Tanya) Martynova, 20, and her friend Yulia Kuprikova, 19, who'd been on a night out together in an Angarsk suburb. The bodies of both women were found at midnight that same evening by a shepherd in the corner of a muddy field on the outskirts of the city.

Tanya's sister and husband Oleg were called by police at 1 a.m. and ordered to attend the local police station without any explanation as to why. When they were finally told what had happened, Tanya's husband Oleg collapsed on the floor and kept repeating: "She was killed, she was killed." The victim's husband and sister were coldly informed by a night duty police officer that both bodies had been found next to each other. They'd been raped and stabbed, and their remains had been chopped to pieces.

That same night, Oleg visited the morgue to identify his wife's body. Tanya's sister recalled: "He felt sick when he saw the body, she was so mutilated. He was almost green when he came out of there – he just could not say a word." Oleg and Tanya's sister later said it felt as though the police didn't really care.

In early December 1998 – just over a month after this attack – Popkov picked up teenager Svetlana Misyavitchus during that snowy night and left her for dead. Her survival convinced some detectives that the attack was not linked to the earlier killings.

Popkov's wife backed her husband after officers questioned her about his whereabouts on the night of the attack on schoolgirl Svetlana. Psychiatrists suggested that this was most likely down to the guilt she felt about having had an extramarital affair and the possibility that she had unintentionally played a role in driving him to attack Svetlana.

However, Popkov's police bosses felt it was necessary to advise him to take early retirement. No one to this day knows if this was directly connected to the murders and the suspicion that he might be the serial killer behind them.

At the end of 1998, Popkov left the police force in Angarsk and became a security officer for a private corporation. He also started buying and selling cars on the side to make some extra cash. Popkov's new job meant he regularly drove between his home city of Angarsk – where his attacks had been carried out – and Vladivostok, on Russia's Pacific coast, a vast distance of almost 4,000 kilometres away.

* * *

Late one evening in July 1999, teenager Evgeniya Protasova's romantic date night in a restaurant ended with a row with her boyfriend as they left the premises in Angarsk. He'd wanted her to go to his home, but 18-year-old Evgeniya refused and insisted that he take her home immediately. The boyfriend was so furious at her rejection that he told her to go home on her own.

A few minutes later, Popkov slowed his car down alongside Evgeniya on a nearby darkened street and offered her a ride home. When she hesitated, he said he was a plain-clothes police detective and showed her his ID card. Popkov advised Evgeniya to accept his offer of a lift home since – as all locals knew – there was still a rapist at large in Angarsk. As Popkov opened the door to his car for her, he struck Evgeniya over the head with his police baton and she lost consciousness.

Evgeniya came to after Popkov had dragged her out of his car and was heading towards some woods. She managed to get free from his grip and ran off through the foliage. Moments later, she tripped over a mossy log. After chasing her down, he would use that same log to smash her over the head until she blacked out. Her last thought, she would say in later interviews, had been: "I'm going to die tonight."

A group of people picking mushrooms found Evgeniya unconscious in the forest the following morning. She was completely naked, with bruises all over her body, but the worst ones were around her neck. Popkov presumed he'd strangled her to death. But somehow she survived, just like his earlier victim Svetlana.

Evgeniya awoke later that day in a hospital bed in the nearby city of Irkutsk. She, however, had a very different disposition to his only other living victim, Svetlana Misyavitchus. She told her friends and family she'd rather try and forget the incident altogether. She put off talking to the police so many times that in the end they gave up trying to interview her. Evgeniya also thought no one would believe she'd been attacked. The police eventually dropped their enquiry. Evgeniya got married and went on to have two children, a son and a daughter.

In many ways, Evgeniya's attitude was a reflection of life in post-communist Russia at that time. Nobody really trusted the police to do the right thing. And as is so often the case, people also didn't want to get involved. Today many say that the Soviet state had knocked the curiosity and independence out of many of its citizens. Under the communists, it had been one of the world's most notorious police states for three-quarters of a century. From Stalin's bloody reign to the less violent but still rigidly authoritarian rules of Khrushchev and Brezhnev, the Soviet police force had always dominated the population. And this attitude still existed throughout the 1990s, despite the fall of communism. The police continued to operate as if they were above the law.

One month after the attack on Evgeniya – on 17 August 1999 – Maria Molotkova, 20, who worked at a water pumping station in Angarsk, was found dead in a forest just 15 miles outside the city after she'd gone missing. The murder wasn't linked to the earlier attacks by police, despite obvious similarities between them.

On 8 June 2000, friends Marina Lyzhina, 35, and Lilia Pashkovskaya, 37, were picked up by Popkov in his car in the middle of the night as they were returning from an evening out on the outskirts of Angarsk. The next day Popkov took an enormous risk by returning to the murder scene having dropped his police identity token on the ground during the attack on the two women. He wanted to retrieve it before investigators discovered it.

Popkov located the token almost immediately and was about to leave the scene when he heard one of his victims still breathing. He clinically finished her off with a shovel and headed home to his wife and daughter. Neither of them commented on the scratches on his face, random blood smears and other signs of a struggle following that 8 June attack.

Over the following 10 years up until 2010, dozens more women were raped and killed by Popkov in secluded spots in Angarsk and the Irkutsk Oblast district. He beheaded one woman and gouged her heart out as he had done during one of his earlier attacks. Popkov often abandoned the naked, mutilated bodies of his victims in plain sight. This gave the impression to some detectives that the killer was actually proud of his murders. As a result, the local media began referring to the still-unidentified murderer as "the werewolf" or the "Angarsk maniac".

He began taking bigger and bigger risks. On one occasion, Popkov murdered a teacher from his own daughter's music school after a meeting with her to discuss making a generous donation to a local charity that helped poor people afford funerals for their loved ones. Popkov later admitted to detectives: "My daughter asked me to give her money, which I did before I killed her." The teacher's corpse was eventually found in a forest close to the body of another of Popkov's female victims, but the former policeman was not interviewed about either murder.

One detective told a local newspaper reporter that police were intrigued by the killer because of the way he seemed able to charm many of his female victims and convinced them to trust him. The detective explained: "Yet the man is a vicious beast inside. It must be like fighting off a werewolf for those women once he launches an attack."

Many women living in and around Angarsk at the time believed that the police's flippant attitude proved that the authorities at that time were not taking the murders seriously enough or that they were hiding something. One woman told a newspaper reporter: "It feels as if some police officers consider this monster just 'a bit of a naughty boy' who seduces loose women and then gives them what they deserve." Popkov adored reading everything about his crimes in the media and later admitted that it convinced him to continue his slaughter of innocent women.

In 2011 – after nearly two decades of indiscriminate killings – pressure finally began being put on the police by state authorities in a bid to try and bring the killer to justice. Police chiefs in Angarsk ordered their detectives to re-examine all unsolved murders in the area.

Investigators matched tracks found at the scene of three of Popkov's early killings with a make of car called a Nova. Officers also recovered what they believed could be identifiable DNA at the scene of those same three murders. They still, though, had nothing concrete linking the killings directly to Popkov. Investigators then concluded that the Nova tyre tracks could well have been from a police vehicle, as so many of that model were used by the city force. But Popkov's name still did not appear on their main list of suspects.

In a bid to try and match up the DNA also recovered, 3,500 serving and retired officers from the region – including Popkov – were ordered to provide DNA samples. That DNA eventually matched up to Popkov's sample. The tyre marks from the Nova police car driven by Popkov were compared to the tracks found near those three earlier victims. They also matched. Detectives also discovered that – despite being described by many as a faithful, solid family man – Popkov had contracted the same sexually transmitted diseases as one of his victims. After 20 years of indiscriminate killings, Popkov was finally his former colleagues' number one suspect.

In June 2012, without his knowledge, detectives put Popkov under surveillance and shadowed him as he set off on a road trip to Vladivostok to buy a car. On a strip of highway outside Angarsk, his vehicle was surrounded by police cruisers and he was stopped and arrested without incident. Popkov stunned police officers at the scene by confessing to 20 murders as he sat handcuffed in the back of a police cruiser at the scene. He proudly told arresting officers that his youngest victim had been a 15-year-old girl.

During his first full interview at a police station following his arrest, Popkov openly admitted to one of his former colleagues: "I never thought of myself as mentally unhealthy. During my police service, I regularly passed medical commissions and was recognized as fit." Popkov admitted with a note of pride that he'd led "a double life". He told his interrogators: "In one life I was an ordinary person … In my other life I committed murders, which I carefully concealed from everyone."

He insisted to detectives that the reason he'd murdered so many women was because he'd been determined to "cleanse" the streets of "prostitutes". He told investigators: "The victims were those who, unaccompanied by men, at night, without a certain purpose, were on the streets, behaving carelessly, who were not afraid to enter into conversation with me, get into my car, and go for a drive in search of adventures, for the sake of entertainment, ready to drink alcohol and have sexual intercourse with me. Not all women became victims, but those of a certain negative behaviour, I had a desire to teach and punish them."

Detectives quickly began pressurizing Popkov to admit to more murders than he had initially confessed to, including the more recent killings committed outside the Irkutsk region where Popkov lived. And investigators were convinced he must have killed other women between Angarsk and Vladivostok.

Within hours of Popkov's confession and arrest, some former police colleagues reacted to the overwhelming evidence against him. One officer told a local newspaper: "When I heard about him I literally choked, because I used to work with him and thought I knew him."

Following Popkov's arrest, detectives approached his survivor Evgeniya Protasova and asked her if she would give evidence against Popkov, as she was one of only two women to have survived one of his murderous attacks. Evgeniya was extremely reluctant. She had never told her husband about the attack. She'd felt the pressure building inside her for years, though, of keeping everything secret from all her family and friends. She eventually co-operated with detectives after admitting she was glad it had all finally come to light and agreed to give evidence against Popkov.

When Evgeniya saw Popkov in an identity parade following his arrest, she was disgusted. Instead of the big, strong monster she remembered, he was a small, skinny man. She told journalists that Popkov should be executed because "a man like that doesn't deserve to live".

When another victim's sister Viktoria Chagaeva saw a photo of Popkov in a newspaper following his arrest she was even more stunned. She realized for the first time that she had met Popkov, the man who had killed her beloved sister Tanya. "I was struck with horror when I saw the picture of this maniac in the paper and online," she explained. "My sister's killer was looking into my eyes. I immediately felt as if I'd met him. Looking at him, I could hardly breathe. Some minutes later I looked at him another time and thought – oh my God, I know him." She had met him in a local bar one night many years earlier. Viktoria was so shocked that she grabbed a knife in the kitchen of her home and frantically cut Popkov's face out of the newspaper.

Viktoria's mother Lubov had died prematurely at the age of 66 in 2007. She'd never been able to cope with the trauma caused by her daughter Tanya's brutal murder. Viktoria recalled: "She felt as if she'd died with Tanya, life became useless for her. She lived only because she was visiting various mediums one by one, looking for the killer and wasting her money. The pain does not go away – it was me who gave Tanya a ticket to go to a concert, and she was killed after attending it."

Popkov told detectives numerous grisly details of his many murders, but it was the detached way he described the rape and killing of one of his most recent victims that most disturbed investigators. During a reconstruction at the actual murder scene, Popkov told police officers: "We quarrelled and I murdered her. I hit her on the top of her head. She fell down and did not show any signs of life."

A photo published in a local newspaper showed Popkov handcuffed to a plain-clothed policeman, with armed officers nearby, demonstrating how he had killed his victim. His face showed no signs of remorse. One detective recalled: "Popkov was very calm when talking to us. And once we confirmed what he'd said, he seemed happy to have been of service."

Popkov showed little or no remorse as he smiled while accompanying the police at further murder scenes, much to the anger of the Russian public, who demanded that the death penalty be reinstated for this monster. Before his trial, Popkov was found by psychiatrists to be legally sane, although the experts pointed out he had a "pathological attraction to killing people".

At the start of Popkov's trial in 2015, he was asked by judge Pavel Rukavishnikov how many women he'd killed. Popkov shrugged and replied: "I can't say exactly, I didn't keep a record." He also told the court: "I admit my guilt in full … [in] committing the murders, I was guided by my inner convictions."

Watching the proceedings was his first surviving victim, Svetlana Misyavitchus, and her mother. She wanted to look him in the eyes and felt that, by being there, she could take any power he still had over her away from him. The moment Svetlana saw the handcuffed Popkov being led into the court-room, her legs buckled and she collapsed to the floor.

Svetlana – by this time aged 37 – appeared in the witness stand and told the court: "His attack aged me by seven years. My brain was permanently damaged. If not for him, I would have had a normal life, had a family, and given birth to great kids."

Popkov remained unemotional throughout most of his trial as it became clear there was overwhelming evidence linking him to many of the killings he'd admitted to. Throughout his many police interviews and trial, Popkov never once confessed to raping his victims – only to the murders. He claimed that any sex he did have with them was consensual and happened before they were dead. Forensic examiners and police investigators had clear evidence that he did rape many of his victims while they were still alive. In Popkov's deluded mind, he believed that he'd seduced those women and was not an actual sex attacker.

He was eventually found guilty of committing 22 murders. During his 2015 trial, the judge and prosecutors revealed to the court that investigators were still looking at an additional 47 deaths, which Popkov had refused at that stage to comment on. The following day, Popkov showed no emotion as he was sentenced to life in prison without the chance of release.

Popkov's wife Elena, 51, and daughter Ekaterina, 30, to whom Popkov supposedly had been a good husband and father, refused to believe he was a serial killer. Elena said: "If he were to be released right now, I would not say a word and we would continue to live together. I love him, I support him. He did not cause me any harm for all these years. I felt safe with him." Elena secretly met Popkov on two consecutive days just before he was sentenced to discuss his situation. She told reporters that her husband already knew he would be given a life sentence. "If I'd suspected something was wrong, of course, I would have divorced him. I supported him, I believed him," Elena said. Observers pointed out that she was speaking publicly about her husband just days before he planned to appeal for a reduction in his life sentence.

Married for more than 30 years, Elena continued to insist Popkov never showed any signs of being a killer and that she and her family had always felt "safe" with him. She labelled the charges against him as "fairy tales", despite his own confession in court about being one of the world's most prolific serial killers. Elena helped write a number of appeals for her husband following his sentencing and visited him many times in prison. She also insisted to reporters that the couple still remained married.

When Popkov's daughter Katya asked her father about the killings during a prison visit after the trial, he told her: "Katya, you understand that all these allegations are fairy tales. It is the system – I have worked within it, I know this system well." Katya had by this time become a maths teacher. She told one TV reporter that she intended trying to solve the crimes for herself to prove her father was innocent. "I do not believe any of this," she said. "I always felt myself a 'Daddy's girl'. For 25 years we were together, hand in hand. We walked together, rode bikes, went to the shops, and he met me from school. We both collect model cars, so we have the same hobby." She added: "Watch how a butcher works, he is covered in blood from head to toe. Did the women lay down meekly by themselves? I bet they would leave marks – bites or scratches. You cannot hide this. But my father did not have any suspicious marks on his body or face."

Popkov's elderly mother also appealed to her son through the media, saying: "Misha [Mikhail], give us some sign if you have done all this or not. And if so, why? It is hard to live knowing nothing. We need to know." In one newspaper interview she said: "I cannot believe he walked alone to the forest in a police uniform. Where was the blood? His clothes should have been covered in blood or if he had tried to wash the blood away, the clothes would have been wet. His wife would definitely have noticed all that. He loves his family, cherishes his daughter, and he dreamt about grandchildren. He would not have done this. He will remain my son, until my death. He studied well and from the very beginning he was an excellent pupil. He loved to cook, pancakes or something like this and he was very neat, like me." Popkov never fully explained why he'd blamed his mother's promiscuous behaviour when he was a child for turning him into a serial killer after his original arrest.

Popkov's sister – also called Elena – described her brother's life sentence as "a tragedy for the family" and echoed her mother's words. She said: "It's hard to even think about this, we are shocked and it causes us pain. There was no violence in our family at all. We just want to know an answer if he did this or not."

Six months after his sentencing, though, Popkov became extremely upset when he was told he'd been stripped of his former police rank, which meant his wife would no longer receive his monthly retirement pension cheque. This decision ate away at him, and in 2017, Popkov asked prison staff to contact detectives, insisting he had something important to tell them. The following morning, he sat down in a private room at the prison with two investigators and announced he was willing to make further substantial confessions to help solve 59 new cases, if his pension was reinstated. No one knows to this day if his wife was indeed paid his pension, but detectives are convinced he murdered more victims than the total of 81 that he took the blame for.

For each new confession, Popkov always provided extremely complex descriptions of the killing but often little collaboration, which meant it could take investigators years to prove all the crimes he committed. Prosecutors themselves suspected Popkov had used the pension issue as a red herring and had deliberately explained the murders in such a method-ical fashion in order to delay his transferral from a standard detention prison to a much harsher penal colony in central Russia to serve out his life sentence. One detective explained at the time: "He names the places where bodies are hidden. We locate these bodies, and check his movements at the time to see if he could have been involved. Then he provides us with crucial details of what he did and when. Then we have to check that evidence to confirm the accuracy and often dig up graves. It's a long-drawn-out process and Popkov knows that only too well." The only cases detectives could hope to clear up speedily were the few where Popkov had left DNA traces confirming his involvement.

Popkov basked in his own weird world of fame and granted interviews to journalists following his sentencing. He informed one reporter he would never have been caught without the invention of DNA. "I could not anticipate DNA. I was born in another century. Now there are such modern technologies, methods, but not earlier. If we had not got to that level of genetic examination, then … I would not be sitting in front of you." Asked what he'd do differently if he could turn back time, he told the same journalist: "I wish my entire life had been different." It was the only time he seemed to openly voice any regret for what he'd done.

In January 2018, investigators announced they'd been able to extract from Popkov confessions to a total of 60 more murders and that they'd charged him with those killings. This meant Popkov's total of kills was now 82, making him the most prolific known serial killer to have operated in Russia during the twentieth and twenty-first centuries. Popkov was eventually found guilty of murdering an additional 55 women between 1992 and 2007 and given a second life sentence.

He went on drip-feeding his murder confessions to detectives and leading police to further fresh kill sites in an attempt to continue avoiding being sent away to the grim penal colony in central Russia, where he was due to stay for the rest of his life. In August 2020, Popkov admitted to a further two murders, and detectives announced that they believed he'd most likely murdered "close to 200" people. As an additional punishment, Popkov was ordered by the judge to serve the first 15 years of his life sentence in solitary confinement. Shortly after this, Popkov was finally transferred to serve that sentence at the Torbeyevsky Tsentral, in Mordovia. It was the very place he'd tried so hard to avoid being sent to.

During the 2020 coronavirus pandemic, Popkov was put to work making face masks in his cell. It was only during this period that Popkov publicly revealed for the first time that he wished Russia still had the death penalty. Popkov told one journalist: "There have been many moments when I thought the death penalty was better. I have a lot to regret. For example, that none of this had happened, that I had not done these things. It is a natural desire of any person – to regret. I have had a lot of time to think about it." When quizzed yet again about the final toll of women he'd killed, Popkov remained typically evasive. He said: "I did not count the number of my victims."

Meanwhile Popkov's wife Elena and daughter Katya eventually moved to another city following a public back-lash against them for refusing to concede that Popkov was a serial killer. It was later publicly disclosed that Elena had fallen in love with one of the police investigators who'd actually helped catch Popkov. In the middle of 2020, Popkov's daughter Katya became pregnant by her husband. She immediately sought psychiatric advice on whether her unborn child would inherit her father's maniacal genes. She demanded that Popkov should be sent for a new psychiatric examination in Moscow but also admitted that she hoped to meet him face to face again one day.

The results of those gene evaluation tests have never been disclosed, and there has been no further news about daughter Katya's pregnancy.

CHAPTER SEVEN

WHATEVER MOTHER SAYS

**Pionerskiy Prospekt, Novokuznetsk,
Kemerovo Oblast, Russia, February 1997**

The smell was so overpowering that an emergency plumber called in by apartment block residents frantically walked up and down the poorly lit corridor of one floor of the building trying to work out exactly where the stench was coming from. So much graffiti had been painted on the walls since the fall of communism that it was hard to spot the front doors to each of the apartments in the corridor.

After two hours, the plumber still couldn't work out where the smell came from but, having served in the military, he had an ominous feeling about what was causing it. He was walking towards the third-floor exit when he heard the noise of someone crying. He kept quiet for a few moments and heard it again. It seemed to be coming from an apartment at the other end of the corridor. As he made his way towards it, the stench definitely got much stronger. When he got to the last front door in the corridor, the plumber stood still for a few moments while he thought about what to do next. Then he heard someone crying again, so he knocked hard on the door. A dog immediately began barking loudly, and it sounded like a big animal.

When no one answered the front door, the plumber leaned against it to try and listen for any sounds from inside. He heard a faint crying noise but then the barking dog smashed against the other side of the door, so he couldn't hear anything except the animal growling, panting and slobbering. The plumber crouched down and gingerly pushed the letterbox open with one finger. The dog snapped at it and he only just pulled his finger away in time.

Then he heard a man speaking from behind the door. The voice told the plumber he couldn't come in because he was sick. The smell coming from the apartment was overpowering by this time. The plumber sighed, as he sensed something was wrong. Someone cried out "help" just before the sound of a window slamming shut.

Moments afterwards, he noticed the silhouette of a man scrambling along a balcony attached to the side of the apartment block through a window at the end of the hallway. The plumber watched the shadowy figure closely for a few moments before the man disappeared out of sight.

Then the dog in the apartment began barking very loudly again. The plumber carefully pushed open the letterbox once more, this time making sure that his fingers wouldn't be protruding enough to have them bitten off by the dog. He could just make out smears and splatters of blood on the walls inside the apartment. The dog was sitting growling up at him. His teeth were bared, and the plumber noticed blood smeared all over the animal's face. Terrified, the plumber turned and ran down the corridor to a public phone on the wall next to the elevator and called the police.

* * *

The police took more than half an hour to get to the apartment block. The plumber was waiting in front of the building chain-smoking when they finally turned up. The two patrolmen listened with grim expressions on their faces as he explained what he'd seen and warned them that someone must have been hurt in the apartment so they should be on their guard. He also told the officers about the man he'd seen on the balcony.

When there was no answer at the door, one of the policemen looked through the letterbox and saw the blood splatters on the walls. The two patrolmen drew their pistols and forced the front door open to be greeted by a huge, hairy Newfoundland hound galloping towards them at full pelt. A shot rang out as one patrolman shot the animal dead.

The officers then heard a sound from the kitchen. So, both guns drawn, they walked tentatively towards it. Two pots were simmering on the stove. When one of the policemen looked more closely at the one without a lid, he noticed a couple of sausages floating in boiling water. It was only as he turned off the gas that the patrolman realized they were human fingers. The other officer gingerly removed the lid from the other, bigger pot simmering next to it and saw that it contained a human head.

They were about to radio in their findings when they heard a noise coming from the bathroom. One officer nodded at his colleague and both men entered it slowly. Inside the bathroom, in a blood-soaked bath, was a child's mutilated, headless torso. A steel tank by the window contained remains of a chest and legs. Then the officers heard a moaning sound coming from another room, the sitting room. They entered it with guns still drawn and found 15-year-old Olga Galtseva. She'd been punctured with multiple knife wounds and was lying on a sofa, which had a plastic sheet over it. She looked slowly up at the two policemen with eyelids soaked in blood and just said: "Help me please."

Paramedics arrived within minutes and rushed the teenage girl to hospital. The two patrolmen were soon joined by dozens of other policemen, who flooded the area to search for the man the plumber had seen escaping along the balcony. Elsewhere in the apartment, other human remains were discovered, as well as in the kitchen refrigerator. This included faces, heads and bones. Children's clothing and shoes were scattered across the floor of the entire apartment.

At the Novokuznetsk General Hospital, doctors frantically stemmed the bleeding from the numerous knife wounds inflicted on schoolgirl Olga Galtseva. She'd lost a lot of blood, especially from two deep incisions in her chest.

Back at the apartment block in Pionerskiy Prospekt street, neighbours told police that the flat belonged to a middle-aged woman, who lived there with her son, a man in his late twenties. There was no sign of either of them.

Two detectives visited the hospital to try and talk to Olga. She was out of surgery and conscious. Despite her appalling injuries, she insisted on being allowed to talk to the officers. What she told them was virtually beyond their comprehension, and centred around her neighbours, Alexander Nikolayevich Spesivtsev and his mother Lyudmila.

* * *

Alexander Nikolayevich Spesivtsev was born in the Siberian industrial town of Novokuznetsk on 1 March 1970. As a child, he was underweight and frequently ill. After his father lost his job at the local steelworks, he turned to alcohol and eventually began abusing his son both physically and sexually. One day – when Spesivtsev was about five years old – his mother and father had a row during which his father beat his mother to a pulp and simply walked out, never to be seen again.

Spesivtsev spent the rest of his childhood consoling his mother, which shaped his entire, nightmarish future. From then on until he was at least 14 years old, Spesivtsev slept in the same bed as his mother Lyudmila, who worked at a nearby school as a teaching assistant. Many who knew them at the time later said Spesivtsev took over the role of his father in virtually every sense of the word.

The pair lived with Spesivtsev's older sister Nadezhda in that apartment on Pionerskiy Prospekt, in the centre of Novokuznetsk. Spesivtsev had few friends during his child-hood, as he was painfully shy and continually bullied at school. Lyudmila encouraged a toxic relationship to develop between herself and her son. She was a domineering personality who believed her needy little boy required her non-stop attention if he was going to make anything of his life. Lyudmila never apologized about anything and refused to take any responsi-bility for her behaviour. These days, she would no doubt be diagnosed as suffering from serious mental health issues, but back in the Soviet Union of the 1970s and early 1980s, no one seemed to care.

Young Alexander Spesivtsev had little to compare his strange childhood to, so he thought it was all perfectly normal. As one of Spesivtsev's few childhood friends explained: "After his father left, he and his mother teamed up to take on the world. They never seemed to care about anyone else and he did everything she asked, without ever questioning it." Spesivtsev knew nothing of rules and morals, since there had been none while he was growing up. He and his mother lived in their own bubble where just about anything was acceptable, as long as they remained welded together.

Having been brutally abused by his father, Spesivtsev interpreted his mother's love towards him as being genuine and extremely protective. As a result, he constantly fed off his mother's approval for every important decision in his life. And when she did get angry with him, Spesivtsev would cower in a corner shaking as he was so worried about upsetting his mother. Sometimes Lyudmila used blatant emotional blackmail to get her son to do whatever she wanted. She would have sex with him as a reward for doing what she ordered. And if ever Spesivtsev hinted at breaking free from his mother's control, she'd threaten to commit suicide. He was completely trapped.

So mother and child were already on a poisoned, downward spiral. Yet despite their mutual neediness, they harboured a lack of respect for each other which, combined with Lyudmila's extreme domination, contributed towards her son's sexual desires.

When Spesivtsev was 12 years old, his mother was fired from her job as a teaching assistant after being accused of stealing plumbing equipment from the school where she worked. In fact, she was running a secret black-market business in stolen goods in order to supplement her low income. Within weeks of leaving her school job, Lyudmila was appointed as an assistant inside the city prosecutor's office. She had access to police files and within a few months was regularly taking crime scene photos of corpses back home to show her young son.

Spesivtsev was startled by the graphic pictures at first but gradually became fascinated by the horrific scenes, which often showed dismembered and slashed bodies of murder victims. His mother even went out of her way to explain to her son about the "beauty of death", as she called it. Spesivtsev soon began storing many of his favourite images inside his head, so that he could think about them while he masturbated. When one classmate at school noticed one of the gruesome photos hidden in an exercise book, he told Spesivtsev that mothers should not be showing their children such images. Spesivtsev beat him up for insulting his mother.

Today, psychiatrists are convinced that Lyudmila showed her son the photos as part of her chilling "education" of him. She was moulding him into doing anything she wanted. Lyudmila knew exactly how to push her teenage son's buttons, since she was the one who'd put them there in the first place.

Spesivtsev's outlet for all these disturbing forensic images was to daub abusive graffiti on the walls of their apartment building. The images often featured dead bodies and satanistic-type proclamations. No one on the housing estate reprimanded Spesivtsev as everyone preferred to keep a distance from him and his domineering mother.

At school, he became much more aggressive with other pupils who tried to bully him, and soon his classmates avoided any social contact with him. When school staff tried to talk to Lyudmila about her son's violent tendencies, she dismissed their fears. Lyudmila informed one teacher that her son was a genius who few understood. It was awkward for the staff to point all this out to her since she'd once worked at the same school, before getting her job in the prosecutor's office. Teachers had recognized serious and dangerous mental problems in Spesivtsev, as well as his mother. They'd noted that he seemed to derive pleasure from hurting other pupils, but Lyudmila refused to get her son examined by a psychiatrist.

Back at home, Spesivtsev became increasingly obsessed with the gruesome crime scene photos his mother brought home for him to look at. He'd study certain images for hours on end, often while sitting next to his mother in the living room and sometimes in the bed they shared.

So while most of Spesivtsev's contemporaries were enjoying all the usual teenage pursuits, he more often than not found himself at home with just his mother for company. As a result, he missed out on many experiences that might have helped him to break free from her spell. Instead, he grew up believing that Lyudmila's demands and desires were completely normal.

Just after Spesivtsev left school aged 17 in 1988, he met a local girl called Evgenia Guselnikova. She was a year younger than him. They soon grew close and had what appeared to be a romantic relationship, which initially revolved around roses, chocolate and poems. Spesivtsev's mother and sister encouraged the relationship and vacated the apartment whenever the pair wanted some time alone. Spesivtsev's sister Nadezhda was by this time working as a secretary to a town judge in the same building where her mother worked.

Lyudmila started to become quite detached from her son's girlfriend as their relationship got more serious. Instead of being happy for him, she was jealous and began criticizing Evgenia in an effort to put Spesivtsev off his girlfriend.

One day, Spesivtsev and Evgenia were alone in the apartment when Evgenia made a rude comment about Lyudmila. Spesivtsev was particularly sensitive to any criticism of his beloved mother and flew into a rage. Evgenia burst into tears. Spesivtsev hadn't seen anyone crying since his mother on the day his father walked out on the family when he was five after beating his mother. So what followed seemed perfectly normal to Spesivtsev. He began hitting his girlfriend and she cried even more. Eventually Evgenia tried to run out of the apartment.

Faced with such blatant rejection for the first time in his entire life, Spesivtsev grabbed his girlfriend and smashed his fist into her face. He then dragged her into a bedroom in the apartment. His mother Lyudmila arrived home soon after this but did nothing to prevent her son locking his girlfriend away. Spesivtsev kept Evgenia trapped in the apartment for weeks. He systematically beat her and humiliated her in every way possible. Lyudmila remained in the apartment throughout and completely ignored the screams and crying coming from the bedroom where Evgenia was kept tied to a bed.

Evgenia's parents had contacted the police within hours of their daughter going missing. Officers were initially reluctant to get involved, especially since one of the policemen they spoke to knew Lyudmila from the city prosecutor's office. Evgenia's parents called round at the Spesivtsev apartment a number of times to try and find their daughter, but no one answered the door, although they were sure they heard noises from inside the flat.

After Evgenia had been missing for almost a month, the police were alerted again by her family, and this time officers raided the apartment, where they found Evgenia tied to a bed, badly beaten and with multiple stab wounds. Spesivtsev had starved her of food and drink much of the time and submitted her to continual, violent sexual assaults. He was immediately detained by police. Lyudmila insisted to officers she'd been away from the apartment most of the time and knew nothing about her son's activities.

Evgenia was rushed to hospital but died within days. Her entire body was covered in so many septic wounds that it was impossible for doctors to determine exactly what had caused her death. The official reason was given as sepsis.

Teenage killer Spesivtsev was not prosecuted by police. Instead, he was committed to a mental hospital, where he was ordered to undergo extensive psychiatric treatment. He was eventually diagnosed with schizophrenia and other mental health ailments. There were rumours that Lyudmila had convinced her colleagues at the city prosecutor's office that she would ensure her son was "cured" without them having to go through the expense and effort of an actual criminal trial and subsequent prison sentence.

Just two years after Evgenia's death in 1991, Spesivtsev was allowed home after doctors said he'd fully recovered and was not a threat to the general public. The paperwork authorizing his release was never actually seen by anyone. Many believe Lyudmila secured her son's release by paying a bribe to a hospital official she knew through her assistant's job at the prosecutor's office.

Such blatant corruption was commonplace in the new, financially destitute Russia. Before the end of Soviet rule, Novokuznetsk had had five enormous steelworks, but they'd all closed in recent years, and citizens lucky enough to have jobs were not usually paid full salaries or pensions. Other penniless citizens set up kiosks on street corners to try and make a living selling anything they could lay their hands on. A local mafia flourished for the first time in decades. No wonder many public officials demanded bribes in order to survive financially.

Also, by keeping her son out of jail, Lyudmila managed to regain control of him. She hadn't really approved of his relationship with Evgenia in the first place but had let it play out, knowing full well how it would end. The Soviet welfare system had collapsed, and social services were not equipped to deal with Spesivtsev. They'd actually recommended that he be released into the custody of his mother after he was released from that mental hospital. And Lyudmila was determined never to let her son out of her sight again.

After his release, Spesivtsev openly admitted to his mother that while he'd been in the mental hospital he'd asked another patient to insert a metal ball into his urethra to make him more virile. But this had had the opposite effect, causing him erectile dysfunction and severe genital pains. Lyudmila assured her son that from now on she'd be in charge of his sex life. She would point him in the right direction.

Spesivtsev and his mother had already concluded that the new democratic regime which had risen from the ashes of communism was a disaster. As a result, Spesivtsev was encouraged by his mother to hate transients and beggars and street children, who she collectively considered to be yet another tainted by-product of Russia's penniless new era of so-called capitalistic freedom. Many homeless children lived in cellars of abandoned houses in the city where they sniffed glue. They avoided adults as most had come from abusive homes, just like Spesivtsev. They also kept out of the way of the police, who were constantly hounding them off the streets. Lyudmila convinced her son that the broken and vulnerable youngsters would make ideal bed-mates for him and that no one would come looking for them like his only girlfriend's parents had.

In April 1996, Spesivtsev met four homeless boys at a local construction site and lured them into his mother's apartment by pretending he wanted them to help him burgle it. He told them he had the keys to the flat. After opening the apartment's front door, he forced all four boys into the sitting room by threatening to stab them. When one of the boys tried to fight back, Spesivtsev plunged a huge kitchen knife into him. When the other children tried to rescue their friend, Spesivtsev stabbed them all in a murderous frenzy and had sex with their corpses.

A few days afterwards, he lured two homeless girls aged 12 and 14 to the apartment by offering them money to work for his new soap-selling business, which he claimed to be running. When they walked into the sitting room, they saw the bodies of all four boys laid out on the carpet. Terrified, the two girls tried to make a run for it, but Spesivtsev stabbed them both with the same knife he'd used to kill the boys.

Mother and son chopped up the bodies of the six young victims. Lyudmila bagged up the remains and dumped some of them in the river Aba, which was overlooked by their apartment block. She also dropped other body parts into buckets and headed out to a wasteland on the edge of town late at night to bury them.

When the severed heads, torsos and limbs of children began to wash up on the banks of that same river, police initially seemed disinterested. Missing homeless children were not high on their list of priorities at that time. Police eventually announced that the remains were most likely victims of organ smugglers, as several gangs were rumoured to be active in the city at that time.

During the month of June, 1996, Spesivtsev killed four more victims – two teenage girls, one woman in her forties and a man of about 35 years old. The last two were never actually identified. They were all murdered, dismembered and their body parts cut up and dumped by Lyudmila. The following month, a 19-year-old called Natalia was killed, and weeks later, two 12-year-old girls disappeared. The police insisted that each person reported missing had run off somewhere and would turn up safe and well.

And in the middle of all this, the Spesivtsev family found themselves suffering financially, like so many of the city's hard-pressed citizens. The police had recently clamped down on black-market racketeering activities, which had seriously impacted on Lyudmila's stolen goods "business". The Spesivtsevs were struggling to afford food for themselves, let alone their fierce Newfoundland dog, so they started feeding some human remains to the animal. Spesivtsev and his domineering mother soon concluded that they might as well eat their victims as well.

So, in addition to beating, raping and murdering innocent human beings, mother and son began slicing up their victims' bodies and cooking them.

And just below the apartment block, more and more remains of children were washing up on the banks of the river Aba. Other body parts were also discovered in a rubbish dump close to the school that Lyudmila had once worked at and her son had once attended. Those earlier claims by police that they were the victims of organ smugglers started to ring hollow when forensic examinations of more than 70 body parts recovered from the river established that most of the remains belonged to children aged between 3 and 14. The sheer number of victims convinced prosecutors that they might have a serial killer on their hands.

In late 1996, the region's Directorate of Internal Affairs deployed several hundred army troops and police officers to begin the hunt for the killer. They had no idea they were dealing with a mother and son "team" at that stage. As squads of armed police supposedly scoured the city to find the person throwing body parts into the river, they never once considered Spesivtsev as a possible murder suspect, despite the killing of his girlfriend in that same apartment overlooking the river back in 1991. In fact, Spesivtsev had not even been flagged up, since there was no paperwork relating to his early release from psychiatric hospital after mother Lyudmila had bribed the hospital's officials.

Detectives decided to target relevant known criminals who'd previously served their sentences in a prison or a psychiatric hospital. During these investigations, detectives had what they considered to be a stroke of good luck. An unemployed man called Oleg Rylkov – who'd committed a series of brutal rapes and child murders in the nearby city of Toliatti – was arrested. Authorities immediately announced that Rylkov was their number one suspect for the murders connected to all those body parts found in Novokuznetsk. Spesivtsev and his mother Lyudmila were delighted when they read about the arrest of so-called killer Rylkov. It was like a green light to the pair to continue murdering innocent young people.

During the winter of 1996/1997, more children were lured into their apartment. Spesivtsev even began picking up older victims in nightclubs and bars, as well as out on the streets. They were always unaccompanied. Inside the Spesivtsevs' apartment, victims were chained up, battered and beaten for long periods of time before they were killed. Lyudmila continued to encourage her son to rape them after they'd died to ensure he was always sexually satisfied. The corpses were chopped up and they fed parts to their dog, as well as cooking meat for themselves. Mother and son liked to let their victims know their fate and keep them alive for a while, so the pair often forced children to eat the remains of their friends before they were also killed.

In the middle of this homicidal frenzy, Spesivtsev's sister Nadezhda periodically visited her mother and brother in the old family apartment. Detectives suspected she must have known that something was happening, but she never reported anything to the police. She later claimed she was terrified her mother and brother would kill her if she told anyone what she'd seen.

Neighbours in the apartment block frequently heard screams and groans but never called the police. They insisted they thought the sounds had been made by Lyudmila's supposedly mentally ill son after his mother had told neighbours he was sick.

* * *

In February 1997, 15-year-old Olga Galtseva went out with her two friends to buy batteries at a shop underneath the apartment block where she and the Spesivtsevs both lived. Outside the store, Olga accidently bumped into Lyudmila, who was weighed down with shopping bags. She and her two teenage friends kindly offered to carry all Lyudmila's shopping home for her. Once inside the apartment, mother, son and their fierce Newfoundland dog trapped the three teenage girls in the sitting room. Lyudmila warned them not to try and leave. When one of the girls did try to flee, Spesivtsev killed her instantly with a knife in front of the others. He then tied up the remaining two girls up and began torturing them while his mother looked on.

The following day, the parents of the three missing girls pleaded with the local police to help try and find their daughters. They were informed by officers that the children had most likely run off with boys. In any case, the police did not have the resources to launch an investigation.

Back inside the apartment, the two surviving girls were ordered to cut their friend's corpse into pieces, so it would be easier for Spesivtsev to hide the remains. He gave them a hacksaw and they did what they were told. He instructed them to make sure they sliced the meat off their friend's corpse in such a way that he and his mother could fry it up like two steaks. Afterwards, mother and son ate big chunks of the human meat in front of the two terrified girls and offered them some of the meat to eat. When Olga's best friend refused to eat the flesh, Lyudmila stabbed the girl until she capitulated and had to eat her friend. Spesivtsev's dog was encouraged to lap at the girl's open wounds while she sat sobbing on the sofa.

That evening, Spesivtsev cut further pieces of meat from the dead girl and her injured friend and flung them at his ever-hungry dog. Spesivtsev ordered the injured girl to carry some of her own cut-off flesh to the bathroom, where strips of it were placed in the bath and a steel tank placed on a window sill. Lyudmila sat and watched all this on a sofa in the living room. She never once spoke directly to the girls and treated them all as if they did not exist.

Just a few yards from the ground floor of the same apartment block, fresh body parts of children began once again washing up on the riverbank. The police still refused to launch an investigation into the missing three teenage girls, insisting to their parents that there was no proof that these were their remains. The bankrupt police force couldn't afford to carry out DNA tests on the body parts at the time.

Back in the apartment overlooking that same riverbank, Spesivtsev beat both surviving girls severely and raped them in front of each other. He broke one girl's hand and left her head bleeding so profusely that Lyudmila sewed her torn skin together with a needle and thread. She wanted to ensure the girl would be fit enough to face more sexual assaults and stabbings from her son.

Olga's severely injured friend was soon further attacked by Spesivtsev, and the dog finished her off by taking chunks out of her face and stomach. Her body was cut into pieces in front of schoolgirl Olga. These were then eaten by mother and son. Olga was stabbed for refusing to eat her friend. She knew she was about to die but wanted to do so with dignity.

It was in the middle of yet another attack on Olga by Spesivtsev that the emergency plumber started knocking on the door following complaints about the appalling smells in the apartment block. Knowing that someone was there encouraged Olga to cry for help, but all that did was make Spesivtsev and his mother more angry. Olga heard another knock on the door followed by Spesivtsev telling the plumber he was ill and so the plumber couldn't come in. Olga passed out. Moments later, Spesivtsev climbed out of the window onto the balcony and escaped.

While the horrified plumber was calling the police from a nearby public phone, Lyudmila slipped out of the apartment, leaving their dog and the unconscious Olga, who was eventually rescued by police and paramedics. From her hospital bed, surviving schoolgirl Olga told police how the man had killed her two friends in the apartment while his mother looked on and then she'd been forced to dismember their corpses. The detectives were staggered by what they heard. Seventeen hours after being admitted to hospital, Olga died.

After raiding the empty apartment, police found a diary written by Spesivtsev and his mother that documented the murders of 19 people. Police would eventually conclude that the pair had most likely murdered more than 30, but forensic pathologists were never able to establish the exact figure.

While searching the flat, investigators found more than 80 items of adult and children's clothing. Much of it was stained with blood. They also uncovered large quantities of stolen jewellery. One detective stumbled on Polaroid photographs of naked and tortured children, some of whom would never be identified. Police also discovered numerous building materials that Lyudmila had been unable to sell after her black-market business was closed down by the police.

Three days after the initial police raid, Lyudmila was arrested by police when she returned to the apartment thinking the police would have been long gone. Lyudmila – by now 60 years old – immediately told investigators about the killings and insisted her son had committed them all. She claimed she'd only helped her son dump the remains of his victims because she believed he might hurt her. In fact, she'd very much been the gatekeeper of his most chilling secrets all along.

Spesivtsev remained on the run, but he wasn't used to life in the outside world away from his evil mother and that stinking apartment. He found himself hungry and in need of a new victim. In mid-February 1997 – five days after escaping from the apartment – Spesivtsev forced a woman at gunpoint back to his mother's apartment. He was about to rape and kill her when police knocked down the front door following a tip from neighbours. Spesivtsev immediately admitted to police who he was and claimed he'd only returned to the apartment to see if his mother was okay. He had no idea that she'd been arrested.

Under police questioning just a few hours later, Spesivtsev confessed to killing 19 children and implied there could be further victims. But few of them could ever be fully verified. Spesivtsev admitted to detectives that he and his mother had been eating victims for the previous five years.

Back out on the streets of Novokuznetsk, a handful of homeless children recounted their close shaves with the man the Russian media had nicknamed "The Cannibal of Siberia". "He came up to me once, but I ran away," Lyosha, an 11-year-old urchin, told reporters shortly after Spesivtsev's arrest. "He was always around. We all knew what he looked like."

At his first court appearance in the early spring of 1997, Spesivtsev confirmed he'd committed at least 19 murders. The judge warned Spesivtsev that if found guilty he would be sentenced to imprisonment for life. Spesivtsev made a point of referring to his mental health problems and began openly refusing to take full responsibility for his crimes, despite his earlier confessions.

Spesivtsev was eventually convicted of just four murders. Police believe to this day that he killed at least 80 people, given their discovery of 82 sets of clothing in the apartment. Spesivtsev underwent a new psychiatric examination, and doctors recommended that he should be kept as an in-patient in the Oryol psychiatric clinic, near Volgograd.

The families of some of Spesivtsev's victims believed that his mother's links to the city's judicial authorities meant investigators deliberately slowed down any subsequent enquiries, as well as allowing Spesivtsev to be declared not mentally fit to face a criminal trial. "The police had no interest in solving every killing because it might expose the corruption that enabled that monster to carry on killing for so long," said one heartbroken mother.

Spesivtsev's mother Lyudmila was sentenced to life in prison with a recommended minimum of 13 years for luring teenage girls for the pleasure of her son, so that he could rape, torture, murder and dismember them. Spesivtsev's sister Nadezhda – despite admitting she was aware of her brother and mother's brutal crimes – was not prosecuted after agreeing to give evidence against both of them. Many victims' families were upset that Spesivtsev's sister was given psychiatric tests and quietly freed without charge.

Lyudmila Spesivtseva was released early from prison in 2008 for "good behaviour" and moved into an apartment with her daughter in the countryside, well away from Novokuznetsk. She has not uttered a word in public since her release. Today, Spesivtsev resides at the Kamyshin Regional Hospital, in Kazakhstan, and regularly undergoes psychiatric tests to see if he is sane enough to stand trial for more of the murders he committed.

When a local reporter was allowed to interview Spesivtsev following his trial, he admitted he still considered human flesh to be edible and a commodity to be traded. As the journalist was about to leave the hospital following the interview, Spesivtsev asked him if he could help organize the sale of his own head. "He thought some institute might want to study his brain after his death and might pay, in advance, in cigarettes," the reporter explained.

Many of the citizens of Novokuznetsk believe to this day that the police's indifference to the killings proves how little they cared about many of the young victims, who might not have been murdered if the police had acted faster. Following Spesivtsev's conviction, police delayed digging for more missing bodies until the snow had melted. Then they quietly dropped the supposed relaunch of the investigation. Lyud-mila Barashkina – whose daughter Zhenya was one of the two 13-year-olds who disappeared with their good friend and final victim Olga – told one newspaper: "We keep trying to see the prosecutor to find out what they're up to, but his secretary just says, 'You're only coming in over my dead body,' and throws us out. And that new investigator … hasn't bothered with us at all."

Others are convinced that Spesivtsev's reign of terror would never have happened if the new Russia had not been in the middle of an economic and social meltdown at the time. Incarcerated mass killer Spesivtsev passes his time writing poems and reflecting on the evils of Russia's new permissive democracy, which his mother had often told him had turned her beloved Soviet world into a violent sin bin of corruption, vice and cheating politicians. Asked by one detective how he could possibly justify his crimes, Spesivtsev answered with a shrug: "How many people has our democracy destroyed? … If people thought about that, there wouldn't be any of this filth. But what can you do?"

CHAPTER EIGHT

GREEN WITH ENVY

Krasnoufimsk, south-west Russia,
Spring 2009, early evening

The newspapers had dubbed the mass murderer in their midst as the "Monster of Krasnoufimsk", a small city with just over 40,000 residents. The old and vulnerable were the favourite targets, as they were easier to control and much simpler to kill.

On this occasion, the killer stayed back in the shadows under a tree watching and waiting for the perfect moment to strike, as had already occurred so many times during the previous five years. The killer usually studied aspects of the target's life in advance, so as to learn their movements and habits, including when they were and were not in the company of other people, in order to calculate the best time to invade their home.

The media referred to the monster as an evil character with dark, soulless eyes and pockmarked skin. One report claimed he walked with a limp. A public appeal by the police referred to the killer sometimes wearing a blonde wig and pretending to be a woman. The killer had laughed especially loudly at that last description, since it was so off the mark. None of the detectives seemed bright enough to realize that the biggest clue of all had been staring them in the face ever since the first attack.

Now hiding in the shadows of a dark alleyway close to the latest victim's house on a cold evening, the killer continued to wait patiently. Most cold-blooded murderers simply pounce when the urge takes them, but this one was very different. The planning and anticipation had become almost as energizing as the kill itself. And no murder was ever a rushed job. After a childhood of waiting for others to grant permission for everything, even to use the toilet, this killer never took anything for granted.

Tactics were changed from time to time, to ensure the police remained confused. In previous attacks, the assailant had gained entry into homes by pretending to be a social worker. This time, a so-called decorator had knocked on a few front doors in the street the previous day to ensure that the presence of such an individual in the neighbourhood would not be considered unusual.

When pensioner Bilbinur Makshaeva opened her front door, she asked the figure standing in front of her to come in almost immediately because of their nice smile and polite tone. Such personality traits were very important to retired teacher Bilbinur, who'd always been a stickler for manners in the classroom. She'd also often taken pity on shy pupils, convinced they were the ones who needed her the most.

After the stranger walked into the hallway, the old lady shut her front door and showed her guest to the neat living room, so they could discuss how much it would cost to decorate the entire apartment. Bilbinur had just mentioned a cup of tea when a hammer smashed down on her skull so hard that her legs buckled and she collapsed onto the floor. The stranger crouched down and began hitting her again with the hammer. By the time the assault was over, there was such a big hole in the old lady's head that a lump of her jellified brain tissue was visible.

The stranger then frantically began scavenging through the apartment, looking for cash to steal. There was none in a sideboard, and jewellery in a box in the bedroom was ignored because the intruder knew how hard it was to sell on stolen goods in the city. The priority was always to find every bank note and coin, so the entire apartment was ransacked. This also ensured the police would presume it was a burglary gone wrong. The assailant claimed not to get any real pleasure from smashing up crockery and sending cupboards crashing to the floor, as tidiness was next to godliness as far as they were concerned.

Just before leaving the apartment, the intruder glanced back into the living room to make sure the old lady wasn't moving. It was always important to be absolutely sure the job had been properly completed. So – grasping the hammer in one hand – the invader crouched down beside the old lady and was about to smash the hammer down again on her head when the noise of children playing in the corridor outside the apartment disturbed the attacker's concentration. A deathly silence filled the apartment as the raider waited until the children were gone from the corridor before slipping out and heading slowly and calmly towards the exit to the apartment block.

A few minutes after this, Bilbinur Makshaeva opened her eyes just enough to see if anyone was close by. When she was sure her attacker had gone, she began screaming for help. She didn't realize it at the time, but she was the only person to ever survive an attack by the so-called Monster of Krasnoufimsk.

The two detectives who turned up at Bilbinur's hospital bedside initially concluded that the battered and bruised old lady had dementia and might have injured herself in a fall, so they insisted on having her examined by psychologists to see if she was of sound mind. The experts rapidly pronounced Bilbinur as being extremely mentally alert. She also passed a set of intelligence tests that would have confused most people half her age. As a result, the two detectives returned to her hospital bedside and got her to repeat everything twice to make sure they wrote it all down and to be certain she was telling them the truth.

Bilbinur was irritated that the police had wasted more than 24 hours by not believing her in the first place. She insisted her intruder had been a woman, not a man as police had labelled the serial killer ever since the attacks started more than 10 years earlier. One detective commented to Bilbinur that no woman could have committed such brutal, senseless attacks. It had to be a man. But she was adamant.

* * *

Irina Viktorovna Gaidamachuk was born in 1972 in the town of Nyagan, in the autonomous region of Khanty–Mansi Okrug, in the sparsely populated eastern heartlands of what was the biggest communist state on the globe. Both Gaidamachuk's parents were alcoholics and drug addicts at a time when Soviet authorities were claiming that their perfect society had no such social problems. There was a vast, secret drug problem in Russian cities at that time. And while the government ignored it, the over-stretched police and social services tried to cope, though clearly they didn't have the time or money to deal with such issues.

The addiction problems of Irina Gaidamachuk's parents had a serious impact on her health, as her mother and father were often not capable of taking her to see a doctor when she was sick. As a result, she developed several serious illnesses during the early years of her life, which left her physically and mentally damaged. Her parents' dependency on narcotics also meant that neighbours often looked after little Irina because she was frequently being left alone at home from a young age. Then – when she reached the age of four – Irina's father began abusing her, both sexually and physically. Throughout this period of her early childhood, Irina's parents' less overcrowded focus remained entirely centred around obtaining drugs and alcohol. Irina was painfully shy and constantly cried in an effort to get some attention, even after her father beat her to try and keep her quiet.

The over-stretched social services department in Irina Gaidamachuk's home town of Nyagan were alerted by a concerned neighbour just after Irina turned five in 1977. Officials informed her parents that they were placing their daughter in an orphanage. Neither the mother nor the father protested, as they were so high on drugs at the time.

Over the previous 50 years, the Soviet Union had built many orphanages to deal with the large numbers of homeless and uncared-for children following wars, droughts and enforced food shortages. They had been notoriously brutal places where abandoned and sickly children were often treated like cattle. By the time Irina Gaidamachuk arrived at an orphanage in the mid-1970s, they were supposed to have become a lot less overcrowded and more relaxed than they'd once been. They'd also been renamed boarding schools to try and soften their image in the eyes of most of the population.

Innocent little Irina Gaidamachuk found herself in one of these establishments hundreds of miles from her family home. She soon discovered that life there was so lonely and the carers so strict that many of the children ran away, preferring to become homeless drifters than to continue to live at the boarding school. Gaidamachuk later said she particularly hated the place as she felt completely alone there. None of her family ever visited her and she had no friends. She did read a lot of books, which she said helped her immerse herself in a fantasy world that revolved around her favourite fictional heroes.

By the time Gaidamachuk reached her teens, she'd already begun secretly buying vodka in a nearby village, which she'd use to drown her sorrows. That was how she learned to understand her parents' need to use alcohol to get through life. And as her dependency on vodka increased, Gaidamachuk started regularly running away from the orphanage. Each time she disappeared, authorities found it harder to track her down. Gaidamachuk often ended up drinking herself into a stupor on a riverbank or joining up with gangs of homeless kids in nearby towns.

After three years of constantly running away – often with other teenagers – and being re-caught and locked down in the orphanage, Gaidamachuk was ordered to leave the estab-lishment and fend for herself. She was just 16 years old. Not surprisingly, Gaidamachuk struggled to find any work or a place to live. She tried to visit her parents a number of times, but they refused to let her in their front door. Her mother hadn't even recognized her the first time she turned up, and it had made no difference when Gaidamachuk had explained who she was.

Gaidamachuk eventually drifted into working as a prosti-tute on the streets of Nyagan. It was the only way she could earn enough money to survive. After a couple of incidents during which men forced themselves on her without her consent, Gaidamachuk decided to leave that part of her life far behind and start again in the town of Krasnoufimsk, located a thousand kilometres away in the Central Urals. She'd saved just enough money from her work as a prostitute to rent a small flat. She even quit the streets and found herself a job in a factory. Gaidamachuk lived in hope that one day a man might come along and rescue her, although she doubted there were any good ones out there after what she'd already been through.

When Gaidamachuk turned 20 in the summer of 1992, she met a man called Yuri. He seemed okay and soon made it clear he wanted to spend his life with her, so they married and Gaidamachuk soon had two children with him. She genuinely believed her marriage and family would provide her with the happiness and stability she'd never known throughout her short life. She desperately wanted to put all those bad childhood memories behind her.

Being a good mother and wife was not easy, though. Gaidamachuk struggled to deal with many of the most mundane aspects of married life. Husband Yuri soon started criticizing her abilities as a parent, and she found that the only way to cope was to start drinking alcohol again to kill the pain.

When Yuri discovered that his wife was spending much of her housekeeping money on vodka rather than food for the family, the couple began constantly rowing.

Krasnoufimsk – the city she'd once hoped would provide her with a fresh start in life – was turning into a prison for Gaidama- chuk. She was trapped with a bad-tempered husband and two children without enough money to buy enough vodka to drown her sorrows. Gaidamachuk tried to get a proper job but since quitting her factory work to have children she'd slipped down the pecking order when it came to employment in the city.

Krasnoufimsk wasn't exactly thriving at that time, either. Back in the communist-run 1960s, tens of thousands of tons of radioactive monazite concentrate had been stored in the city. This contained thorium, which was used in nuclear weap- ons. The facility was closed down after demand for thorium declined. Then, following the downfall of the Soviet Union, tens of thousands of residents fled the city to live elsewhere after a rumour started that they could get cancer from the radioac- tive fallout from the monazite still stored on their doorstep.

Back in Gaidamachuk's family home, she still somehow managed to function as an effective parent, despite the drink- ing and her husband's suspicion of her. She became very skilful at hiding alcohol from Yuri, but it wasn't easy. Gaidamachuk made a genuine effort to behave well in front of her husband's relatives, friends and neighbours, though. She knew Yuri was watching her every move, to try and catch her secretly drink- ing. Gaidamachuk's addiction to vodka soon became more blatant, and her husband began forbidding her from going out. Often, she could barely stand up, although she continued to insist she could look after their children. He doubted it. Yuri was holding down a full-time job and finding himself looking after the children whenever he was at home. Not surprisingly, he began refusing to give Gaidamachuk any money. She said she'd tried to get a job, but they both knew she could never hold down a job if she remained a drunk.

And throughout all this, Gaidamachuk continued to be haunted by memories of her toxic parents and their rejection of her. She lived in fear that her own children would end up being taken away from her. This made her incredibly anxious, and alcohol provided a release from that mental pressure.

Eventually – in desperation – Gaidamachuk returned to her old profession of prostitution. It was risky work. Many of the men who paid her for sex were violent and she was often left battered and bruised. But she needed to feed her vodka habit and contribute towards the upkeep of the children. When Yuri found out what she was doing, he threatened to throw her out of the house unless she stopped immediately. He warned her that he would never allow her to come back if she ever went back to selling her body again.

Gaidamachuk later claimed that her husband's threats cut through her like a knife, and she began to feel he was betraying her just as badly as her parents had done when she was a child. She particularly loathed the way people – including her husband – disapproved of her drinking more strongly because she was a woman. She thought that was deeply unfair.

Inevitably, Yuri's family began to notice what was happening to his marriage. One time, Gaidamachuk randomly informed one of her husband's relatives that women were just as capable of violence as men. The relative took this as an insult to her. After the incident, Yuri rounded on his wife and accused her of being drunk, so she stormed out of the family home.

Gaidamachuk began to realize that a lot of her problems lay in her childhood. She undoubtedly needed professional help but felt helpless as she didn't want to tell her doctor in case the children were taken away from her. So her only way to forget those appalling memories – albeit temporarily – was to continue to drink. The only time Gaidamachuk went out was when her husband was at work and the children were at school. On those occasions, she would wander aimlessly around the shopping areas of the city dreaming about what it might be like to be rich.

In June 2002, Gaidamachuk was walking through one of Krasnoufimsk's less rundown neighbourhoods and noticed an old lady struggling to cross the road carrying several heavy shopping bags. Gaidamachuk offered to help her, and the woman asked her in for a cup of tea after they arrived at the front door to her apartment. Gaidamachuk was delighted to be appreciated. Moments after walking into the old lady's apartment, she noticed expensive paintings on the walls and valuable furniture and found herself feeling very jealous. Why did this old woman have so much more than her?

Gaidamachuk tried to block out those feelings of envy. The old lady then kindly offered her a vodka to warm herself up with. The impact of the alcohol instantly transformed Gaidamachuk's personality. Moments afterwards, she picked up one of the old lady's expensive vases and smashed it over her head, knocking her unconscious. Gaidamachuk rifled through the old lady's belongings in the apartment until she found the equivalent of £20. It seemed like a fortune to her. She was about to leave the flat when the old lady regained consciousness and shouted at Gaidamachuk that she was going to call the police.

With that, Gaidamachuk smashed another vase over the victim's head, knocking her out. Gaidamachuk headed into the kitchen where she found a hammer in a drawer. She returned to the living room and hit the old lady's skull a dozen times until she was definitely dead. Gaidamachuk later described how she was shaking with excitement at this point. "I felt strong and powerful for the first time in my life. It was a nice feeling, even though I knew what I had done was wrong," she recalled.

Within an hour, Gaidamachuk was back at home with Yuri and the children, having announced that she'd just been given a £20 advance after getting a new job at a nearby factory. Gaidamachuk knew only too well that that shot of vodka had completely distorted her outlook on life and turned her into a murderer. But why should she care if no one cared for her? That same night – after she'd read some colourful bedtime stories to her children – Gaidamachuk decided she'd start regularly burgling old people's homes. After all, that first one had been so easy. She felt happier just thinking about it.

The following morning, Gaidamachuk took her children to school and went off to "work". She'd packed a hammer and a bottle of vodka in her handbag and headed on foot to a district of the city where many old people lived. It didn't take long before she spotted an old lady. She followed this one all the way to her apartment, which was in a tidy, residential housing block, the type that Gaidamachuk and Yuri so longed to live in but couldn't afford.

Gaidamachuk stood in the shadows overlooking the entrance to the apartment for some minutes to see if anyone else was in the flat. Then she took a large swig of vodka before knocking on the front door. She charmed her way into the elderly woman's home and once inside she crushed the pensioner's skull with her hammer before stealing all the cash she could find. She'd realized following that first killing that it was better to murder her victims than risk them identifying her, which would have meant being taken away from her beloved children, just like she had been from her parents.

Gaidamachuk found it easy to target new victims while walking around the city's wealthier areas, which had their own busy shopping precincts. During 2003, she followed many of them to where they lived and established their movements before making an approach. Most elderly citizens were creatures of habit, which made them much easier to attack.

Sometimes Gaidamachuk would sidle up to them in busy supermarkets or out on the street and strike up a friendly conversation. Then she'd either accept their offer of a cup of tea or ask if she could use their bathroom.

Irina Gaidamachuk always carried that hammer in her bag. Sometimes she'd have a bigger bag that contained a small axe, which she found was better at killing her victims more quickly. Her priority was always money and food. She remained convinced that jewellery and other personal items would be much harder to sell on the black market.

Towards the end of 2003, Gaidamachuk began sometimes pretending to be a social worker, which was ironic considering her background. She'd learned a lot about them during her childhood and genuinely believed she had the tools to be a real social worker, though she'd never passed enough exams at the orphanage to get there.

Gaidamachuk's furious brute strength when she attacked victims helped lay a false trail for the police, as the killings were so vicious that detectives assumed the murderer had to be male. Detectives were confused as to how the attacker was able to gain entry into victims' apartments so easily. Following the first couple of killings, Gaidamachuk began to deliberately dress very neatly, so that her victims wouldn't hesitate to allow her into their homes. She also perfected good manners and an educated accent, which she combined with a pleasant smile, knowing full well that that was how a social worker would act.

At least half a dozen pensioners were slain in their own homes between 2002 and early 2004, yet the police continued to insist that the killings had been committed by a man. Gaidamachuk recalled: "Each time I read the police saying that in the newspaper, it convinced me to be even more brutal, because then the police would continue thinking I was a man." In thinking this way, Gaidamachuk had managed to gather the brute strength needed to so viciously rain hammers and axes down on the skulls of those innocent pensioners. "Yes, feeling like a man seemed to give me immeasurable power and a sense of bravery. I simply wasn't scared," she explained. In Gaidamachuk's mind, she was also getting her own back on the men who'd ruined her life by blaming one of them for the murders. She liked the way that suspects – all male – were being hauled in and interrogated by police.

And while also working on her violence, Gaidamachuk continued to work on improving her manners to ensure her latest elderly victims fell for her charms.

She would watch each victim with even more attention than the last. This included shadowing them to the shops or the bank or even sitting near them in a local café as she drank a cup of tea and treated herself to a cupcake. Gaidamachuk later admitted that this build-up added a further layer of excitement for her. Knowing she'd soon be hammering this latest victim to death gave her a sense of control.

In the spring of 2004, a witness came forward and told police that they'd seen a strange blonde woman near the apartment of one of her victims. The police soon dismissed the claims and reiterated yet again in the local press that the murderer was a man. They went so far as to insist the killer had clearly pretended to be a woman to throw them off the scent. Not long after this, one detective told reporters that the killer might actually be a transsexual who got a thrill out of pretending to be a woman.

In the middle of all these brutal murders of elderly ladies, serial killer Gaidamachuk and husband Yuri started to get along much better. Yuri had been suspicious at first that his wife had been lying about having a proper job and feared that she might be working secretly as a prostitute again. Gaidamachuk was able to assure him truthfully that this was not the case. In the end, Yuri believed her, as she seemed so much happier than when she'd worked as a prostitute. Gaidamachuk continued using some of the cash she stole to secretly drink alcohol, although for the moment she managed to hold herself together enough to perform her duties as a parent. She even began sometimes helping out at her younger daughter Anastasia's school.

Gaidamachuk later claimed that her improved mood was down to the confidence she derived from the power and control her killing spree was giving her. She lapped up all the stories about her crimes published in local newspapers. Gaidamachuk convinced herself that the attacks were committed by another "version" of her, which meant she wasn't, strictly speaking, responsible for them. When she was out alone prowling the streets for a new victim, she was no longer the gentle, loving mother who had a quiet life at home with Yuri and their children.

There were moments of doubt, though, when the normal, law-abiding side of Irina Gaidamachuk reminded her that eventually the police would begin to inch closer to finding her. But usually she quickly pushed those thoughts out of her mind and retained a steely determination to continue her "job". Gaidamachuk later admitted that by 2006 – four years after her first attack – she was not even afraid of the idea of a full-blown manhunt with helicopters, armed snipers and ground troops. In many ways, she longed for the excitement of a few close shaves, because it would make her feel more important.

But in reality, the police continued to struggle with the case. Part of this was down to the fact that the majority of officers had been trained by the previous communist regime, who didn't have the funds or enthusiasm for proper training so tended to be unable and unwilling to investigate the murders of a bunch of old people who were going to die soon anyway. So most detectives in Krasnoufimsk believed they had more important crimes to solve.

In early 2008, Gaidamachuk daubed the number of her latest victim on the wall outside her home after she'd killed her. Even after she did the same following the murder of her next victim, the police failed to step up their efforts to bring the mass killer to justice. Not surprisingly, local citizens – especially old folk – were becoming increasingly petrified by the failure of the police to investigate the attacks properly. Gaidamachuk recalled that writing the number of each kill on a wall near a murder scene was her way of showing the police she was in control. She said that each time she got away with yet another killing, she felt like there was nothing anyone could do about it.

Detectives shrugged their shoulders and blandly informed local reporters that the monster was numbering each victim to try and get caught. They still had no idea the killer was a woman. A couple of more diligent police investigators pointed out to their colleagues and superiors that the murders had clearly been carefully pre-planned and were not as random as they had been projected by the media. But at no time did any of them realize that the killer's feminine intuition was helping her stay one step ahead of law enforcement.

Back home with her husband and two children, Gaidamachuk continued contributing towards the housekeeping and was able to afford enough vodka to get her through each day. In her head, Gaidamachuk had a genuine job, which no doubt helped her sound more convincing whenever husband Yuri questioned her about work. Gaidamachuk's "real" job was proving just as time consuming as working in a factory. And she'd often watch her would-be victims for days, and sometimes weeks, before actually pouncing on them.

Gaidamachuk had found something she was actually very good at for the first time in her life. And the more she killed, the more she prided herself on not getting caught. She recalled during one interview that it felt to her as if she'd taken on the entire male police force and made them look stupid. She became so confident of escaping justice that she started leaving notes on the front doorsteps of some would-be victims' homes in order to gain their confidence. One such note later found by police informed an intended victim: "Be home at 11.00, a social worker will visit." Gaidamachuk enjoyed playing such games. She particularly liked to gain the trust of people and turn into a monster in front of their very eyes. They had been stupid enough to trust her and now they had to pay the price.

The city's hard-pressed police eventually became so desperate to solve the case that they approached a psychic to try and track down the serial killer in their midst. The only concrete information they knew about the case at this stage was that the victims were aged between 61 and 86. They continued to believe the killer was a man. The psychic used by the police proved as clueless as the detectives had already been. Her only conclusion was that the killer was a man, and an old one at that.

In the summer of 2008, Gaidamachuk murdered an old woman in a small village called Achit. She stole the equivalent of £50 in cash after ransacking her victim's apartment. Detectives were particularly puzzled by the relatively low amounts of cash stolen from victims. Some raids had netted the killer as little as £20 and the most ever taken was just over £300. Why would any professional criminal bother killing victims for such small sums of money? But Gaidamachuk didn't care as long as she had enough cash to contribute towards her family's housekeeping costs and her consumption of cheap vodka.

In the middle of 2008, the police resorted to more desperate tactics by announcing plans to interview 3,000 men with "relevant" criminal records and ties to the region. Gaidamachuk read about all this in her local newspaper with mild amusement, as it seemed such a random way to try and find a serial murderer, and it clearly implied they had little to no idea who the killer was. In any case, the police were only targeting men.

Police responded angrily when rumours began circulating the city after the local press reported one witness saying that the attacker might be a woman after all. One detective angrily retorted to journalists: "There is no way this killer is female. No woman could be as violent. Females simply do not attack innocent elderly people. It's not in their genes." When Gaidamachuk read that quote, she became even more confident she'd never be caught, so felt she might as well spread her net wider and begin targeting elderly people she actually knew personally. And she wasn't worried about being connected to these crimes, especially now she'd decided to set fire to her victims' homes after killing them.

But by the end of 2008, Gaidamachuk's blatant over-confidence began leading to her taking some unneccessary shortcuts. She became more reckless and, in a few instances, careless. During one attack, someone walked into an apartment moments after Gaidamachuk had battered the elderly female owner to death. She just managed to escape out of a window before being spotted. On another occasion, also in late 2008, Gaidamachuk was refused entrance to an apartment by a suspicious old woman who called the police as soon as Gaidamachuk had left. Officers dismissed her concerns on the basis that the person who'd knocked on the elderly lady's front door had been a woman. This close shave seemed to diminish Gaidamachuk's appetite for killing, and she decided it was time to stop before she got caught.

But after months of struggling with her family and her drink problem, she got so desperate for money that she decided it was time to return to "work". In the spring of 2009, she attacked elderly Bilbinur Makshaeva in her home. It was the first time she had failed to kill her victim, after being interrupted by those children playing in the corridor outside her apartment. In hospital afterwards, the old lady insisted to detectives that her attacker was a woman, not a man. For the first time, detectives were now able to issue an accurate description of the killer in their midst, although it didn't actually encourage anyone to come forward with any more evidence. Many believe that the police tried to play down the revelation that the killer was a woman, although they now knew it to be true, as they were embarrassed that it had taken them so long to find out.

Some detectives tried to suggest that a female killer would be less cunning and that that would lead to her making mistakes. They also believed that a woman would feel more remorse for her crimes than a man. Gaidamachuk was irritated when she read in the press that the police finally knew the attacker was a woman, because that would make it much harder to get away with killing any more victims. The local press had not mentioned that her most recent victim, Bilbinur Makshaeva, had in fact survived and that that was why police finally knew her gender.

But despite this new revelation seemingly making Gaidamachuk's life harder, she actually had an incredible stroke of luck. After the police interviewed 3,000 further men and women with criminal relevancy to their investigation, detectives arrested a 29-year-old woman called Marina Valeyeva. According to detectives, she'd immediately confessed to all the killings committed by Gaidamachuk, who was naturally relieved when she read about the arrest in her local newspaper. Valeyeva's confession had been taken from her by two detectives who were veterans of the Soviet era, when torture was often used while interviewing murder suspects.

Now Gaidamachuk had a new incentive to continue killing. She decided to widen her killing zone to include the region that ran south from Ekaterinburg down to Serov, 300 miles away. She believed this would confuse the police following the other woman's arrest.

In early 2010, Gaidamachuk knocked on 81-year-old Alexandra Povaritsyna's front door and claimed to be a professional decorator. After getting into the old lady's apartment, she pulled a hammer out of her bag and smashed it into Alexandra's skull at least three times. This time, however, Gaidamachuk tidied up the old lady's apartment after she'd turned a lot of stuff upside down trying to find cash, so as to confuse the police. Officers who searched the flat less than 24 hours later, after the discovery of the old lady's body, concluded that this might not be the work of the murderer they'd been hunting for such a long time.

At Krasnoufimsk police headquarters, officers re-examined the evidence against number one suspect Marina Valeyeva because she'd been in custody when the murder of Alexandra Povaritsyna had been committed. It was then that senior officers learned from an underworld source that the arrest of their number one suspect Valeyeva had all been part of a plot to frame her by an ex-lover, who happened to be acquainted with some of the police officers who'd arrested her in the first place. The police withheld this revelation from the press in the hope that the real killer might think she was in the clear and make a mistake.

Detectives went back and re-examined all the transcripts of the 3,000 interviews with all the women that they'd carried out more than a year previously. They were hoping to find clues they might have missed the first time around. They also re-interviewed neighbours of Gaidamachuk's last murder victim, 81-year-old Alexandra Povaritsyna, who'd been killed in the summer of 2010.

Investigators wrote down every single detail of the killer's description from those neighbours before creating a photo-fit likeness of the female suspect. For the very first time, they now had a description of Gaidamachuk: a blonde woman in her late twenties. Armed with this, the police produced a vague photo-fit poster, a copy of which was published in the local media. The accompanying news article referred to how the killer gained entry into old people's apartments by pretending to be a decorator or social worker. It was the first time detectives had openly linked all the killings and made a tacit admission that a serial killer might be responsible.

The resulting publicity struck fear into the city's residents, but it made many far more diligent when it came to watching out for any likely suspects. Just five days after that photo-fit was published, police received an anonymous tip from a woman whose elderly neighbour had told her she was about to hire a woman to decorate her apartment. Police had already had dozens of such calls and were reluctant to follow up on the tip without the caller identifying themselves. But when the informant described the "decorator", who'd also knocked on her door, detectives decided it could well be the killer.

An hour later – on 10 June 2010 – detectives knocked down the front door to the old lady's flat after hearing screaming from inside. They found Irina Gaidamachuk and her bag containing an axe and a bottle of vodka. She had been just moments away from killing her next victim. Gaidamachuk was immediately arrested and put in handcuffs. She refused to comment on any of the accusations being made against her by police officers. Some detectives wondered if Gaidamachuk was the vicious serial killer they'd been hunting for nearly 10 years. She seemed too much like an ordinary mother and housewife to them.

As Gaidamachuk was led away to a police van parked up outside the apartment block, she looked down at the ground despite jeers from some of the residents watching the drama unfold from the balconies of their flats. At the same time, two detectives visited the school that Gaidamachuk's children attended. Teachers told investigators that Gaidamachuk was a responsible mother who often helped out in the classroom of her youngest daughter Anastasia.

On that afternoon in June 2010, Gaidamachuk was examined by a psychiatrist in a cell at a local police station. The expert afterwards assured investigators that – although she showed some "variation" in the mind – she was legally sane. Shortly after being told about the results of that examination, Gaidamachuk was also informed by detectives that her fingerprints had been found at the scene of a number of the murders she'd committed. Gaidamachuk sighed heavily and told detectives sitting across a table from her that she had a lot of "stuff" to get off her chest. She began describing all the details of what had happened and insisted on telling investigators the actual addresses where many of her killings had been committed.

At the end of her first interview following her arrest, Gaidamachuk told detectives: "I did it for money. I just wanted to be a normal mum, but I had a craving for drink." She also tried to blame her husband Yuri for not giving her any money to buy vodka. In her warped mind, Gaidamachuk had convinced herself that her supposedly cruel husband had turned her into a mass killer.

Newspaper reporters flooded the area where Gaidamachuk and her family lived and even tracked down one of her few friends. The housewife told journalists: "I simply cannot believe Irina is a mass murderer. She was a kind and gentle mother, always eager to help."

Back at Krasnoufimsk police station, Gaidamachuk was eventually charged with 17 counts of murder and one attempted murder, but detectives had little doubt she'd killed twice that number during a killing spree that had lasted at least 10 years. Finally, police were able to publicly announce they'd caught the city's most notorious mass murderer. They deliberately avoided mentioning that they'd never have known the murders had been committed by a woman if it hadn't been for the little old lady who survived the attacks.

* * *

In February 2012, Gaidamachuk's trial was held at a court in Yekaterinburg – Russia's fourth biggest city. By this stage, she'd retracted her original confession to police and was refusing to admit to her crimes. The court was told that despite her addiction to vodka, Gaidamachuk was neither unclear nor stupid. On the contrary, prosecutors said, she proved to be a shrewd, cold and calculating serial killer. Gaidamachuk's defence lawyer insisted that she was an affectionate and kind mother who would help anyone in need and that this meant she could not have committed such heinous crimes. But when Gaidamachuk was allowed to speak in court, she sounded cold and confident and gave the judge and jury the clear impression that she had known exactly what she was doing by becoming a mass murderer.

On 12 June 2012, Gaidamachuk – by now 40 – was sentenced to 20 years in prison. The judge said he exempted her for 5 years of the maximum 25-year sentence because "she is a mother". The relative of one of Gaidamachuk's murder victims said after the sentencing: "It's little more than one year for each murder. She deserves to never be freed."

After the case, defence lawyers argued that Gaidamachuk should have got a more lenient sentence thanks to her "extenuating circumstances", including all the childhood abuse and neglect she had suffered. The judge eventually rejected Gaidamachuk's appeal on the basis that she had known exactly what she was doing and had been careful to make sure her husband, children and friends never found out she was a mass murderer. Gaidamachuk's husband Yuri said after the sentencing: "I lived with her for 14 years but never suspected anything."

It was then revealed in the local media that husband Yuri had moved away from Krasnoufimsk and begun a new relationship immediately after his wife's original arrest. He has never visited Gaidamachuk in prison.

Gaidamachuk will be 60 years old when she is finally released in 2032.

CHAPTER NINE

LEAVING TAMARA

Apartment block, Dimitrova Street, Frunzensky District, St Petersburg, Russia, summer 2015

Senior citizens Tamara Samsonova and Valentina Ulanova both knew what it was like to suffer. They'd been through difficult, neglected, Soviet-style childhoods and been abandoned by their husbands. But in 2015, they found each other and became the best of friends. Both old ladies lived in the same apartment block in the heart of what had once been one of the city's most innovative housing estates back in the 1970s, when it was known by its Soviet name of Leningrad. By 2015, the brickwork was crumbling and the front doors to each apartment were scratched and battered, but Tamara, 68, and Valentina, 79, didn't mind as they had each other's back.

In March that year, Valentina hadn't hesitated when Tamara had asked if she could stay at her apartment while her home was being redecorated. Within days, the pair were out shopping together, sharing all the housework and regaling each other with stories of the past – both good and bad. Tamara even began calling Valentina by the name Valya because she reminded her so much of her beloved aunt of the same name from when she was growing up in Uzhur, in the Krasnoyarsk Krai region of the then Soviet Union. In the evenings, the two old ladies sat in front of Valya's TV set and laughed and cried together as they watched their favourite soap operas.

Tamara felt happier than she'd ever been. She'd struggled with loneliness for most of her adult life and always found it especially hard when her friends and tenants in the apartment block moved on. Now she had a friend, Valya, who would never abandon her because they lived in the same apartment. Tamara hadn't ever before thought it possible to be so content in the company of another person.

So when the two men painting Tamara's apartment took a lot longer than scheduled to complete the work, Tamara explained the situation to Valya, who told her friend to stay as long as she wanted. Tamara was greatly touched by her friend's unconditional kindness towards her. She later said she went to sleep each evening safe in the knowledge that Valya would be there for her when she woke up.

Neighbours noticed at the time how much happier Tamara seemed to be. She'd had a reputation in the apartment block for being grumpy, but now she was more upbeat and there was usually a broad smile on her face. Whenever neighbours bumped into Tamara and Valya in local shops the pair of them were always laughing loudly together.

Tamara was so content that she began writing a diary about her life at the time. The first thing she put in it was a reference to how happy she felt sharing Valya's home. She sweetly wrote: "I love Valya." Other diary entries included inane phrases about the mundane side of her life such as: "Slept badly", "Drank coffee", "Take medicines" or "I do not eat". Another insert read: "I woke at 5 a.m. Then I do work around the house." Tamara wrote in her diary the day she went out to buy marshmallows from her local baker to give to her best friend. The diary gave the impression Tamara was afraid she'd miss something important in her life if she didn't pour out every single detail. It was clearly an outlet for her true feelings. The strangest thing about Tamara's diary, though, was that she wrote it in three different languages, German, English and Russian, all of which she spoke fluently.

Tamara became so immersed in the diary version of her life as well as her affection for Valya that she failed to notice her best friend grating her teeth with irritation when Tamara didn't bother to clear up dishes after dinner some evenings. At first, Valya's annoyance didn't last long, because Tamara would bake her a delicious cake or cook a fine stew, using ingredients usually paid for by Valya because Tamara was broke. She had a tiny pension from when she'd worked in the hotel trade.

And until the apartment had to be renovated, Tamara had made some extra money by having tenants living in the spare bedroom. But they never seemed to stay long.

* * *

A few months after moving into her friend Valya's apartment, the two old ladies went out shopping together and arrived back overloaded with food and some new clothes, all of it paid for by Valya. After unpacking everything, the two women sat down for a cup of tea and Valya coughed awkwardly before telling her best friend: "I am tired of you."

Tamara was stunned. At first, she continued sipping from her cup of tea as if Valya hadn't said anything.

"I said I'm tired of you," she repeated. "I want you to leave and go back to your own place. I want to be on my own."

Tamara still didn't respond. Instead, tears began rolling down her cheeks. She tried to wipe them away, but they kept coming. Valya handed her a tissue and the two old ladies sat there in silence for some minutes.

Tamara recalled: "I was scared of living at home on my own. I felt panicked and close to fainting with the stress of it when she said that." She looked up to see how Valya was responding to her floods of tears. Her friend was looking, stony-faced, directly at her.

"Stop all that," said Valya irritably. "I am serious. You have to leave."

"Can I stay just a couple more days while I get my flat straightened out?" asked Tamara.

"Okay. But no more than a couple of days. D'you understand?" replied Valya.

That evening both women avoided each other. Tamara cried herself to sleep. She was devastated by what had happened. Why, she kept asking herself, do people not like me? Why? When Tamara woke up the next morning of 23 July 2015, she prayed that Valya might see things differently. Over breakfast, Valya repeated to Tamara that she had to leave the apartment as soon as possible. Once again, Tamara said nothing. This time she didn't cry, either. Instead, she stood up in silence, put her coat on and left the apartment. Once outside, she headed to the nearest railway station and caught a train to the suburb of Pushkin.

Tamara visited a pharmacist she knew in Pushkin and persuaded her to sell her over the counter a prescription drug called phenazepam for her anxiety. Tamara had taken it before and hoped it might make her feel better. After arriving back in Dimitrova Street, Tamara popped into the local grocery store beneath their apartment block and bought the ingredients for an Olivier salad, one of Valya's favourite dishes. Then Tamara popped into her own apartment to pick up some things before returning to Valya's place.

That evening, Tamara was preparing the salad in the kitchen when her friend Valya walked in. Tamara later explained: "She sneered at me and said that making her a salad would make no difference and I still had to leave." After Valya went back into the sitting room, Tamara got a pestle and mortar out and crunched up at least a dozen phenazepam pills and sprinkled them in the salad. She hesitated for a moment to consider what she was doing. Then she poured 30 more tablets into the pestle and mortar and crunched them up until they were also like powder.

Within minutes of eating that salad, Valya fell off the kitchen chair unconscious. Tamara stood up and looked down at her on the floor with a satisfied expression on her face. Tamara retired to bed feeling much happier.

At 2 a.m., she woke up with a start and thought she heard some movement from the kitchen. She knew exactly what she had to do next. In the kitchen, her best friend Valya was still out cold. Tamara decided to drag her into the bathroom as it would be easier and less messy to deal with her in there. She was far too heavy, so Tamara went back into her bedroom and took a hacksaw out of the bag she'd brought with her from her own flat earlier. She'd borrowed the hacksaw from a neighbour at least 10 years earlier.

With her best friend unconscious but still breathing, Tamara started sawing off her head. Valya did not stir and bled out very quickly. Once the head was completely severed, Tamara turned her attention to Valya's arms and legs, to make it easier to carry her body into the bathroom. She placed all the body parts in the bath so that the blood would drain away more easily. Tamara then used two of Valya's kitchen knives to cut her friend into multiple pieces, to make it easier to dispose of her.

Tamara wasn't finished yet, though. She took some of the same human remains back into the kitchen, including the head and hands. She deliberately boiled the hands in order to remove the fingerprints and prevent identification of her victim. She also placed the severed head in a large saucepan and left it simmering.

A few minutes after this, Tamara sat down at the kitchen table and wrote in her diary: "I killed my tenant Volodya today."

Two hours afterwards, Tamara wrapped all Valya's identifiable body parts in some old curtains she found in a cupboard before placing it all in thick black plastic bags. CCTV footage seen afterwards clearly showed Tamara leaving the apartment block in a blue raincoat carrying those bags and returning to take out a saucepan. Tamara dumped the remains in different parts of the Frunzensky district where she and Valya lived. This included in a pond at the end of Dimitrova Street.

Tamara went outside a total of seven times that night with bags containing her friend's body parts. Tamara dumped one bag containing Valya's hips and legs in a neighbour's back garden. She also left a few shopping bags containing smaller body parts around the apartment to remind her of what she'd done. That evening, an exhausted Tamara sat down at the kitchen table and wrote in her diary: "Now I can live here in peace for another five months, until her relatives turn up, or somebody else."

Valya's decision to reject her friend's companionship had cost her her life, but she wasn't the only person to pay the ultimate price for leaving Tamara.

* * *

Tamara Mitrofanovna Samsonova was born on 25 April 1947 in the town of Uzhur, in the Krasnoyarsk Krai region, in the then Soviet Union. Uzhur's economy revolved around a well-developed agriculture system and a railway line, which provided the essential supply chain for all local products. Every type of crop grew there and there was also cattle and sheep breeding. Most of this was exported to the rest of Russia via the railway. Uzhur was also home to the 62nd Missile Division of the Soviet's Strategic Rocket Forces. This was a typically secretive communist-inspired base, which local residents were encouraged not to talk about.

Winters in Uzhur were harsh, and with the area in steep economic decline by the 1960s, many younger residents harboured plans to live elsewhere, once they were old enough. After graduating from the local high school, Tamara moved to Moscow where she studied at the city's prestigious State Linguistic University. She left college after three years fluent in English and German and then moved to the city of Leningrad, where she married a university professor called Alexei Samsonov.

In 1971, Tamara, aged 24, and her husband settled in a newly built panel apartment at number 4 Dimitrova Street, on the eastern side of the city. It was one of more than two million new homes constructed at that time as part of a vast Soviet home-building programme following decades of war and severe hardship. This brand-new residential development was similar in some ways to the classic suburbs of the United States. Although the Soviet leaders at that time would never admit it, they'd replicated the lifestyle and maybe even the suburban attitudes of their biggest enemy. These new housing estates were called "microrayons" (literally micro-regions), and many had a population equivalent to entire cities in the Western world.

The streets of the brand-new estate where Tamara and her husband lived were lined with trees. The roads were properly surfaced and their apartment block even had a large garden in front of it. Tamara and her husband Alexei were considered a sophisticated, highly educated couple by most of their new neighbours. She had a job in the hotel trade, thanks to her multi-lingual talents, and he was an up-and-coming professor at a local university. Tamara had an extensive knowledge of world affairs, which was unusual in Russia at that time.

However, she found the sterile environment of the suburb where she lived very flat and soulless at times. Few neighbours talked to each other much and Tamara often felt isolated when her husband was working long hours. So the couple's supposed dream home meant little to her, as she had no friends in the area. Tamara engaged in non-stop conversations with work colleagues but failed to communicate with anyone in her neighbourhood.

All the apartments had been built in identical blocks, on identical streets, arranged around identical quad formations that stretched as far as the eye could see. It felt to Tamara that the development deliberately crushed any sense of individualism. Tamara later went so far as to describe the suburb where she lived as "hell on earth".

Eventually, Tamara got a much more prestigious job at the Soviet government-run Intourist travel agency, thanks to her multi-lingual skills.

Her new position included working as a liaison officer between her agency and foreign tourists visiting Leningrad, who usually stayed at the city's Grand Hotel Europe. The long hours of Tamara's new job led to Tamara neglecting her marriage to Alexei. She struggled to get pregnant and an awkward void began to emerge between them.

For more than 10 years, the couple struggled on in the hope that once they started a family, it would help them improve their relationship, but Tamara sensed that the distance between herself and her husband was widening. By the mid-1990s, Tamara and Alexei had become virtually like strangers, often working different hours from each other. At home, both tended to prefer reading a good book to having a conversation. Not surprisingly, the atmosphere became flat and empty inside the apartment, as each conducted their life separately from the other.

In 2000, husband Alexei announced he'd fallen in love with someone else. Tamara was devastated, despite the obvious problems in their relationship. Alexei gave her no chance to try and mend the marriage and a few days after that left the couple's suburban home. He was never seen again.

Tamara immediately reported her husband missing to the local police. She insisted he hadn't left her and did not reveal to officers his earlier confession of an affair. The police said that he must have run off with someone and that Tamara should move on with her life. Tamara did eventually admit to neighbours that her husband had indeed run off with a new woman, but she never told the police this.

Those same neighbours soon noticed that Tamara became much more isolated after her husband disappeared. She began to take an interest in black magic after telling one work colleague that she was trying to contact her husband through the spirits. She wasn't sure if he'd ended up in heaven or hell. Tamara later insisted she'd sought the help of a psychic after feeling guilty that her husband had decided to leave her. But she also explained something strange to a work colleague at the time: "I also want to find out if he forgives me for what I did to him," she said. Tamara never explained what she meant by this.

Within months of her husband's sudden disappearance in 2000, Tamara Samsonova's mental health began to deteriorate.

Whether this was down to her guilt or genuine heartbreak will never be known, but Tamara ended up being hospitalized three times over a period of six months and eventually lost her job. Despite her extensive multiple linguistic skills, Tamara never got another job due to those mental health problems that had led to her being hospitalized. Instead, she found herself trapped in her large apartment on a small pension, alone and no doubt extremely depressed. For almost two years she struggled on. Those who saw her at this time said she was suffering both financially and emotionally.

Finally, in the late summer of 2002, Tamara decided to try and make some additional money and find some much-needed company. She began renting out rooms in her flat.

One of the first tenants was 44-year-old Sergei Potyavin. He rented a room for almost a year until the day of 6 September 2003, when he informed Tamara he was leaving to go back to his family, who lived hundreds of miles away in central Russia. Samsonova was heartbroken at the news, as she'd enjoyed their conversations together. She hated the thought of being alone once again and angrily accused Potyavin of abandoning her.

He was so shocked by her embittered reaction that he decided it would be best if he left that same evening and headed to his room to pack his bags. Just moments after this, Tamara went into the kitchen, grabbed a long carving knife and burst into Potyavin's room, where he was folding his clothes. Tamara stabbed him to death in a frenzy before he had a chance to fight back.

That evening, Tamara dismembered her tenant's corpse and disposed of it in some garbage bags, which she dumped on the street near her home.

The remains of a headless, armless and legless man's body were eventually found in various plastic bags dumped near Tamara's street. They were never linked to Tamara in any way at that time. And no one ever came looking for her tenant Sergei Potyavin, either.

Tamara quickly replaced him with two male lodgers. When they announced after just a few months in the spring of 2004 that they were also leaving, Tamara was so upset at being abandoned that she drugged their supper with tranquilizers. After they'd collapsed into unconsciousness, Tamara calmly cut their bodies up into pieces, just like the previous tenant.

Over the following seven or eight years, other tenants came and went. No one knows to this day how many of them there were and if any of them ended up being disposed of by Tamara. But neighbours such as music teacher Maria Krivenko, 53, noticed at least a dozen tenants coming in and out of Tamara's apartment. Maria – who lived in the same block as Tamara for 15 years – recalled: "We saw a few younger people living in her flat. I once asked Tamara why she didn't find a job instead of renting a room and she said she was sick and had medical papers to prove it, so this was the only way she could supplement her pension."

And some of Tamara Samsonova's habits became very eccentric over those years. She'd often go out to the nearest shops in a dressing gown, even in winter. She always bought food and provisions at night because, she told neighbours, that was when she preferred to eat. Tamara informed some neighbours that strangers kept breaking into her apartment when she was out and that they'd cut up all her clothes. That was why she was so often out dumping plastic bags in refuse bins. When one neighbour suggested she should call the police, Tamara hesitated before insisting the police were useless and wouldn't be able to help, so it wasn't worth contacting them. Neighbours also noticed that Tamara's conversations could be very erratic. Sometimes, she'd happily chat about normal things but suddenly switch to "sounding crazy" about men trying to break in to her flat and rape her.

By 2014, Tamara had become virtually unapproachable as far as most of her neighbours were concerned. She fell out with an old school friend called Anna Batalina, who lived in the neighbourhood. Anna said that Tamara turned against her for no apparent reason and told her: "I'll kill you. I'll cut you to pieces. I will throw the pieces out for the dogs. Don't make me angry."

Tamara bizarrely informed Anna that she was capable of anything and that she'd been under suspicion for killing her mother-in-law more than 20 years earlier. Tamara refused to elaborate on what she was referring to.

In the late spring of 2015 – following this exchange – Tamara moved in with her neighbour Valya while her flat was being redecorated and her mood lifted. She told neighbours she felt she'd finally found a proper companion. Tamara assured herself: "She won't abandon me like the others."

But by the middle of the summer of that same year – 2015 – Valya had signed her own death sentence by daring to suggest to Tamara that she should leave her apartment.

* * *

A couple of days after Tamara murdered her supposed best friend Valya, the old lady's friend and neighbour Natalia Vasilievna decided to call at her apartment because she was worried that Valya hadn't been seen for days. Tamara answered the door and invited Natalia in while insisting Valya had simply gone away "for a few days". In the kitchen, Natalia immediately noticed Valya's mobile phone and landline handset on a table and, when she looked more closely, she saw that both devices had run out of battery power and were dead. Also spread out on the same table were her old friend's identity documents, including her passport.

Natalia Vasilievna asked Tamara where Valya would have gone without her travel documents. Tamara repeated that Valya had simply gone away. She admitted to Natalia that she was planning to stay on in the apartment while her friend was gone. Then Natalia asked Tamara if she thought Valya was dead. Tamara hesitated for a moment before explaining:

"Well, just before she left I did get up to make tea at 2 a.m. and found Valentina unconscious with a drink lying on the floor of the corridor outside the flat."

"What happened to her?" asked an incredulous Natalia.

"Oh I went inside to drink my cup of tea and when I went back into the hall, Valya had gone."

Natalia said her heart sank after Tamara said that. She recalled: "I knew something was seriously wrong but I had no evidence that Tamara had done anything, so I just had to leave." That afternoon, Natalia reported to the police that her friend was missing. A social worker was dispatched to Valya's apartment to try and assess Tamara's mental state. Tamara refused to let the woman into the flat.

On 27 July 2015, police officers spoke to residents in the apartment block after finding human remains inside plastic bags near the apartment block and discovering that Valya had disappeared. When officers knocked on Valya's apartment, this time Tamara opened the door, with a smile on her face, and invited them in.

Inside the flat, the policemen almost immediately noticed traces of blood in the bathroom. They also recognized the curtains, which matched the ones that had been used to wrap those body parts in. Tamara was arrested on the spot. She didn't look in the slightest bit surprised, and before they'd left the apartment she began confessing to the killing of her best friend Valya and the three tenants.

Tamara was taken to the nearest police station while other officers searched her own apartment in the same block. They almost immediately found Tamara's bizarre diaries written in German, English and Russian. They were on a shelf alongside books on astrology and black magic. The diaries clearly detailed the killings she'd already confessed to carrying out, including the murder of those three men who'd rented rooms from her. Then police officers read her final entry in the diary. It said: "This is no way to live. With this last murder I closed the chapter."

Some newspaper reports claimed Tamara admitted to up to 10 separate murders in that diary. There was no concrete evidence of these killings, so it was impossible to verify if she was telling the truth. Tamara's diary did also mention a male torso found in her street 12 years earlier, which detectives concluded was most likely a reference to her missing husband.

In Tamara's apartment, police also found a saw and a knife, which, along with those blood spots on bathroom tiles, provided forensic evidence that she had indeed murdered at least three people. The saucepan containing Valya's head – which Tamara was carrying when her image was captured by a CCTV camera at the back of the apartment block – was never recovered. She'd dumped it in a waste disposal container, which had been picked up by a garbage truck that same morning.

Police sniffer dogs did eventually find some of Valya's dismembered limbs in a bush near to the street where both women lived. A headless torso with only one arm and one leg was also discovered in the nearby pond. Detectives suggested that Tamara ate some of the body parts of the people she'd killed, but she adamantly denied this, insisting she only boiled the remains to ensure they were not identifiable.

Following her confession to police, Tamara told investigators she'd once been an actress and was a graduate of the prestigious Vaganova Academy of Russian Ballet. There was no evidence to back this up, and police concluded that she had lied to them in the hope it might ensure the judge at her trial would be lenient to her. One detective recalled: "She's either much more stupid, or much smarter, than she seems."

On 28 July 2015, Tamara was finally officially charged with three counts of murder. She remained in custody in St Petersburg while Russia's Investigative Committee, the country's equivalent of the FBI in the United States, analyzed all the allegations in her diary, which included references to murdering at least 11 people.

Police re-examined other unsolved murder cases involving victims being dismembered and their body parts later found strewn around the city. The wasteland site opposite the block of flats where Tamara had lived for 40 years had recently been developed into more residential apartment blocks, so it was impossible to recover any remains she might have buried there before its construction.

While preparing the prosecution case against Tamara, detectives got her to agree to show them exactly how she had killed

Valya and the three tenants they knew about, in order to provide further evidence of her guilt, as psychiatric experts were beginning to doubt her claims due to her fragile mental condition. Investigators produced a dead pig and asked Tamara to cut it up in exactly the same way she'd disposed of her best friend Valya. They even let her use the same type of hacksaw she'd borrowed from her neighbour's house years earlier. In front of the stunned police officers, Tamara carefully and expertly removed various body parts from the pig. The detectives present that day had absolutely no doubt she'd done it before.

Tamara's first court appearance at the Frunze District Court in St Petersburg on 29 July 2015 was to decide if she should continue to be held in custody ahead of her eventual trial. Tamara sat all alone in the big, draughty courtroom looking up and smiling sweetly as lawyers and other officials walked in. With her sparkling brown eyes and bird's nest hairstyle, many found it impossible to believe that this friendly-looking pensioner with a warm smile was a cold-blooded killer.

When the clerk of the court asked Tamara if she wanted a glass of water, she thanked him politely for the offer and looked around again to see if anyone else was watching her. Shortly after this, half a dozen journalists took their seats behind the attorneys, and the 68-year-old glanced across at them curiously. When one of them – a handsome man in his late thirties – smiled back, Tamara looked delighted and blew him a kiss. Another reporter also smiled in her direction. She put her hand across her eyes and played peek-a-boo with him, until one of her court-appointed defenders leaned down and whispered something in her ear and she stopped. One reporter commented: "She seemed so happy to be there. It was weird when you consider what she'd done." Tamara then turned her attention towards the public gallery, where she recognized a number of people who were friends and neighbours from the apartment block where she lived.

Later that morning – after all the charges had been read out in court – Judge Roman Chebotaryov asked Tamara if she wished to say anything. She first responded: "It's stuffy in here, can I go out?" She then took a long, deep breath and told the judge: "You know I've been preparing for this court action for dozens of years. Everything was done deliberately to bring me to this place…" The judge asked her: "I am supposed to keep you in custody. What do you think?" She replied: "You decide, your honour. After all, I am guilty and I deserve punishment."

Tamara openly admitted everything in court, even how she'd boiled the severed head and hands of her final victim after sawing up her body. When the judge eventually told the court she was going to be held in custody, Tamara smiled and clapped her hands. It later emerged that for years before her arrest, Tamara had boasted to friends: "I will be popular and famous", telling them that one day she would cause a "sensation".

The biggest surprise of the hearing, though, was that one of the male tenants who detectives presumed had been murdered by Tamara turned out to be alive. The court was told he'd informed police he'd be willing to appear as a witness at Tamara's trial as he had had to leave his room in Tamara's apartment after feeling threatened by her.

Within days of her first court appearance, newspapers were alleging that Tamara had a penchant for gouging out and eating lungs, but none of that was true, either. The killings, she later claimed, were all about her loneliness, not her appetite for human flesh.

Three months after that first court appearance – on 26 November 2015 – Tamara agreed to a forensic psychiatric examination at the prison where she was being held ahead of her full trial. Experts concluded that she was a danger to society and herself, and so she was placed in the Kazan Psychiatric Hospital of Special Purpose to undergo compulsory psychiatric treatment. To get there, she had to make a 950-mile journey east in a specially guarded train. It was the same institution where Josef Stalin's much-feared secret police chief Lavrentiy Beria used to shut away political prisoners during the Soviet Union's brutal postwar era.

At the Kazan Psychiatric Hospital, officials announced that Tamara was actually suffering from paranoid schizophrenia and was not mentally fit enough to be dealt with in criminal court. This meant she never actually faced trial for the deaths of the 10 people that investigators ultimately believed she had killed, including her own husband. Those cases have remained in open files ever since.

EPILOGUE: HELL ON EARTH

**The Black Dolphin Prison, near Russia's southern
border with Kazakhstan, December 2020**

This notorious and isolated penal colony was first opened as
a jail back in 1745. Many prisoners insist there are still faint
smears of the blood of its first inmates on its walls from that
time almost three centuries ago. The prison's official title is
the Federal Governmental Institution, and it is run by Russia's
Penitentiary Service. Its nickname comes from a prisoner-
constructed sculpture depicting a black dolphin, which is set
in front of the main entrance.

Since 2000, the Black Dolphin has been home to approximately 700 inmates, all of whom are serving life sentences,
guarded round the clock by more than 900 guards and prison
staff. The jail's current residents are believed to have killed
more than 4,000 people between them. Only one man has
ever escaped from here, and he was cut down by a hail of

bullets in an icy river just hours after tunnelling his way out in the middle of the night.

All inmates arrive here blindfolded. Whenever they're moved from building to building within the prison compound, they're also handcuffed. This ensures they walk bent in half as they're escorted by expressionless prison guards. These inmates include cannibals, serial killers, gangsters, terrorists and paedophiles. They all have one thing in common – they've committed murder.

No wonder the Black Dolphin is reputed to be one of the world's most inhospitable prisons, although staff and some inmates insist the harsh regime inside this grim compound's battered walls serves a purpose by being the ultimate deterrent. Others – including some of the Black Dolphin's most hardened inmates – say they'd prefer it if the Russian justice system brought back capital punishment as it's more humane to many of those who will never be released during their lifetime.

Each inmate is permitted 90 minutes a day of exercise, as long as they have not been banished to solitary confinement, where the cells measure 10 by 8 feet. Prisoners are fed soup and bread four times a day and there is no TV anywhere in the prison. Books, newspapers and magazines are, however, allowed. "To call these inmates people, it makes your tongue bend backwards just to say it. I have never felt any sympathy for them," guard Denis Avsyuk explained in a recent interview.

Some of Russia's serial killers are so terrified about being locked up in the Black Dolphin that they confess to more killings than they were originally prosecuted for in order to slow down the justice system enough to postpone their arrival at this chilling penal colony. This tends to happen after the trial judge orders that part of their punishment should be to spend the first 15 years of their sentence in solitary confinement inside the Black Dolphin. That means little or no meaningful contact with anyone else. At the time of writing, at least half a dozen Russian serial killers were waiting to be despatched to the prison for exactly these reasons.

Other "guests" incarcerated at the Black Dolphin currently include at least three of Russia's most notorious serial killing cannibals, as well as assorted mass murderers. This includes an inmate who butchered five members of his own family before burning their bodies in a forest. There are also professional criminals such as a Russian mafia member who orchestrated a wild Moscow shootout which left seven people dead and eight others injured. This gangster was asked recently by one visitor how he coped with life inside the Black Dolphin. He said: "It would have been better if I'd died with them. You ask me if I would do it again? I've thought about it. To be honest, I probably wouldn't do it again."

At the time of writing, this mobster's own father was scheduled to arrive at the Black Dolphin imminently, after also being sentenced for his role in the same slayings. In a dingy cell four doors up the corridor from where that same gangster resides is a former head of security at an oil company, imprisoned for murdering four men who worked for a business rival. The inmate also happens to have once been a KGB officer in the old Soviet regime.

Another lifer inmate summed up the mental strength needed to survive in the Black Dolphin when he said: "The most important thing is to avoid becoming embittered. It's so easy to turn into an animal here. But staying human is harder. That's why we try – both with each other and with the administration – to stay human."

The Black Dolphin's inmates receive little or no psychiatric care, despite the nature of their crimes. To many, this is a sad reflection of the way most murderers are dealt with in Russia, even today. One eminent psychiatrist, however, rose above the nation's apathy towards its chilling plague of serial killers. Professor of psychiatry Aleksandr Bukhanovsky treated at least a dozen of the serial killers that the nation has actually acknowledged to exist during the past 50 years. Three of them came from his home city of Rostov – a community the size of the UK's Manchester – including Andrei Chikatilo, whose story is featured in this book.

From the early 1990s, Bukhanovsky – then in his fifties – worked alongside detectives and created profiles which helped bring some of Russia's many serial killers to justice. Following their arrests, Bukhanovsky was also permitted to spend long periods of time in their draughty prison cells. There they told him of the unspeakable horrors they'd caused while he tried to dig deep into their inner psyche.

"Why Satan chooses so many of his servants is not for us to question," Professor Bukhanovsky once explained when asked why his home country had so many serial killers. "The problem of serial murder exists everywhere in Russia as well as inside my home city Rostov."

Bukhanovsky controversially alleged that serial killers didn't actually want to commit murder, but often spent decades resisting the final act of killing as it grew like a slow form of cancer within them. He also declared that multiple murderers were often triggered to kill by one specific, disturbing childhood incident. He explained: "A serial killer begins developing from childhood. A psychopath goes through stages before they literally taste blood, and each stage is brought on by different pressures."

Despite his understanding, almost sympathetic mentality, Bukhanovsky was no "soft touch" when it came to the manipulative psychopaths he encountered. He insisted his experiences of dealing directly with them helped him work out if they were sane and fit enough to stand trial. Many remain convinced to this day that Bukhanovsky had a better understanding of serial killers than anyone else in his troubled nation and possibly the world. But his unorthodox methods of treatment for these criminals didn't always meet with the state's approval. They did regularly accuse him of being too soft on them.

In the late 1990s, Bukhanovsky upset Rostov authorities by setting up his own clinic in the centre of the city specifically to study serial killers and other criminals who feared they were on the verge of murdering people. Bukhanovsky provided his medical services free of charge in order to encourage them to visit his clinic. The professor explained at the time: "We're fighting to find the roots of social aggression, and to establish ways to curb it. We are also trying to make people more aware of the problem and encourage sufferers to come forward and not just let their anger grow."

Bukhanovsky infuriated Rostov's law enforcement agencies by refusing point blank to inform them in advance if any killers sought out his advice so that the authorities could arrest and prosecute them. "I have invited many young men in the city who show all the symptoms of becoming serial killers to come and see me on the promise that I will not tell the police," Bukhanovsky explained back at that time. "How else can I get them to attend? If they knew I was going to hand them over, they would not come and they'd continue to kill." One serial killer told reporters following his own capture: "I know that if I'd met Bukhanovsky before I killed, I would have been cured. I'm 100 per cent sure of it."

Bukhanovsky defied authorities by communicating with one on-the-run serial killer by exchanging letters with him. When the alleged killer eventually disappeared, Bukhanovsky was blacklisted by Rostov's police chiefs, who were angry that he had never told them he was talking to the killer. They also disapproved of his openness about the problem of serial killers in the city and across the entire nation, on the basis that it went against official policy.

Bukhanovsky's clinic in Rostov remained open until he died in 2013 of natural causes. Local police and city officials continually threatened to raid the premises while accusing Bukhanovsky of harbouring serial murderers and potential killers.

He summed up his own attitude when he once said: "It is the human condition to exist in a state of natural balance. There are saints to whom we build shrines to honour the goodness of their work. But when I read about a saint, what I cherish is the power of virtue besides the deafening blackness that humankind is also capable of."

Bukhanovsky and a number of other criminologists believe that many of Russia's most prolific serial killers actually wanted to be caught. But the nation's law enforcement agencies were simply too inefficient, indifferent and corrupt to ever acknowledge this, and rarely brought them speedily to justice. As a result, hundreds – maybe even thousands – of people have died at the hands of these psychopaths, who should have been tracked down much sooner.

Re-examining those cases has made it blatantly clear that some were indeed crying out for help to end their addiction to murder. The ultimate proof of this is the way that many of those featured in this book confessed to their crimes immediately after they were arrested. It's as if they wanted to lift the weight from their shoulders. There are no excuses for what these killers have done, although it has been essential to examine their characters closely in order to prevent another generation of killers from following in their homicidal footsteps.

What is fascinating is the stream of cannibalism that runs through these stories. History has undoubtedly left an irreversible residue of it in the DNA of many citizens through no fault of their own. However, it seems from some of the cases featured here that eating human flesh crossed over from being a survival instinct to becoming a way to extinguish the lives and souls of victims.

Russia's famous writer Aleksandr Solzhenitsyn wrote in his 1970s classic *The Gulag Archipelago* how common criminals escaping from Stalin's brutal Soviet gulags (work camps) would often take a "softer" political prisoner, known as a "cow", to eat on their way to freedom if the going got tough while they were on the lam.

Meanwhile Konstantin A. Bogdanov – a folklore expert at the Russian Academy of Science – attributed many of Russia's cannibal cases to a society rooted in Marxism. Bogdanov explained: "Marx believed that people always interacted socially, as classes or groups. When people here want to find a way to manifest rage against their surroundings, they express their deviance socially. And what could be a purer form of antisocial behaviour than eating people?"

Criminologist Dr Adrian Raine believes that biological and social factors both contribute to the making of virtually all murderers. In his book *The Anatomy of Violence*, Dr Raine explained: "Genetics and environment work together to encourage violent behaviour. Anyone with a specific variant of the enzyme monoamine-oxidase-A gene is more likely to display violent behaviour, especially if they've had an abusive childhood." Federal Bureau of Investigation (FBI) serial killer profiler Jim Clemente put it more bluntly: "Genetics loads the gun, their personality and psychology aim it, and their experiences pull the trigger."

Many of the serial killers featured in this book targeted those they felt had rejected them, discriminated against them or somehow persecuted them. This mentality still exists in Russia due in part to the country's immense suffering, which has had a chilling effect on the emotional condition of its citizens.

But do these emotive issues make such heinous crimes any more forgivable?

Wensley Clarkson, 2021

ACKNOWLEDGEMENTS

To all the law enforcement agents who helped me with this book – both still serving and now retired – I offer my eternal thanks.

Then there are the families of many of the victims, who have done nothing to deserve the anguish and heartbreak they will suffer for their entire lives due to the brutal actions of so few.

And finally, I would like to thank the many other experts trying to provide some of the answers about how and why these serial killers murdered in cold blood in the hope that it might help prevent similar tragedies in the future.

I know I have to be destroyed.
I understand.
I was a mistake of nature.

– Russian serial killer Andrei Chikatilo